Living Large

LIVI
LAR

FROM **SUVs** TO **DOUBLE Ds,** WHY GOING **BIGGER** ISN'T GOING **BETTER**

Sarah Z. Wexler

ST. MARTIN'S PRESS

NEW YORK

Portions of "Chapter 3: Saline and Silicone, Supersized" were originally published in *Marie Claire*.

www.stmartins.com

Book design by Jonathan Bennett

ISBN 978-0-312-54025-8

First Edition: November 2010

10 9 8 7 6 5 4 3 2 1

CONTENTS

Living Large

INTRODUCTION

On February 9, 2009, in his first news conference after taking office, President Barack Obama declared, "The party's over." And was it ever. Home foreclosures were at record highs. Americans owed more money and had less in savings than at any time since the Great Depression. Banking giants were collapsing, along with the Big Three automakers. General Motors, one of the largest companies in the United States, filed for bankruptcy. The economy was in a downward spiral, unemployment was skyrocketing, the cost of living was on the rise but consumer spending was at a lull. Depending on which talking head you listened to, America was quickly sinking into a "recession," a "financial crisis," a "crisis of confidence," or a "flat-out catastrophe." Americans had been guilty of living large—accumulating huge amounts of (it turns out apocryphal) wealth in the pursuit of supersizing our homes, cars, businesses, and food portions. But we'd also been living large in the sense of our conspicuous consumption, spending and acquiring so far beyond our means in the '90s and early '00s that, following in the way of any parable, it inevitably led to a massive emotional and financial crisis.

The only upside to such a crisis is that it can lead us to reevaluate everything. So reevaluate I did. Instead of sleeping, I started spending nights pacing around my living room like I was Ben Bernanke himself instead of a former hippie and magazine journalist who usually spent her time writing about trends in books and movies and celebrities or the runway return of harem pants. Still, like most of us, I wondered how—or in my more terrified moments, *if*—America would come out of this. But the more I thought about the future, the more I realized I needed to look back to what got us into this mess in the first place. I started by researching the events of the past few years—just one small part of America's long history of booms and busts—in terms of our individual consumption, and what the pursuit of excess could tell us about what America will look like when we pick ourselves up, dust ourselves off, and decide what's next.

There's nothing necessarily wrong with our living large, nor anything particularly new about it. After all, we're the nation that took Manifest Destiny, the constant quest for expansion, as a call to action. We made the Louisiana Purchase, one of the largest land acquisitions in the history of the world, snapping up 828,800 square miles, almost a quarter of the country. Any number of quintessential American moments can be read as an extension of that view, of claiming more, more, more. But with the days of blatant imperialism over, there's not much frontier left (short of annexing Mexico). So are we Americans feeding that same old urge by claiming space and expanding as individuals—our waistlines, our portion sizes, our houses, our cars? From the Gordon Gekko '80s until roughly 2007 reigned an era of unchecked individual imperialism.

There's no doubt that America is obsessed with size, and also that it possesses the resources to go big. The United States is the world's third-largest country by size (after Russia and Canada) and also by population (after China and India), yet it comes in first for innumerable world's largest records. Namely, we have the most billionaires in the world, filling 45 percent of the slots on *Forbes'* World's Billionaires list. We have more big, wealthy companies than any other country in the world, 140 of *Fortune's* Global 500 list (next behind us is Japan, with less than half that number). We have the world's largest imprisoned population, with 2.3 million people behind bars. We have most of the world's largest roadside attractions, like Salem Sue, a 12,000-pound fiberglass cow sculpture that stands thirty-eight feet tall and fifty feet wide in New Salem, North Dakota, and the world's largest jack-in-the-box, soaring fifty feet in the Middletown, Connecticut, air. ("In many parts of the country, you can plan an entire road trip where you visit nothing but 'world's largest' attractions," says Doug Kirby, coauthor of *Roadside America*.)

We have the world's largest obese population. According to the CIA, we're the world's largest consumers of cocaine. We're home to the world's largest office building (the Pentagon, which spans thirty-four acres). We have the world's largest building, measured by volume (Boeing's factory in Everett, Washington, is 472 million cubic feet and covers nearly a hundred acres). We have Walmart, the world's largest retailer. We have Philadelphia City Hall, the world's largest government structure, at 548 feet high. We built the world's tallest monument, the Gateway Arch in St. Louis, standing at 630 feet tall. We have the world's largest sports stadium, the Indianapolis Motor Speedway, which can hold 250,000 spectators.

As for transportation, we have more airports than anywhere else in the world, plus the world's two busiest, Atlanta's Hartsfield-Jackson and Chicago's O'Hare, which boast the greatest numbers of passengers passing through. We have more roads than anywhere else in the world, paved for 3.98 million miles. We have the most railroad tracks (more than 140,000 miles) and the train station with the largest number of platforms (Grand Central Terminal has sixty-seven platforms, compared to the second largest, Paris's Gare du Nord, with forty-two). MTA New York City Transit has 468 stations, more than any other subway system in the world.

The United States imports the most toys, cars, bicycles, tractors, televisions, pearls, live animals, art, pharmaceuticals, bananas, pineapples, undergarments, shoes, oil, natural gas, aluminum, rubber, furniture, and nuclear reactors. We have the largest gross domestic product and the largest gold reserves, but also the largest national debt.

The U.S. military has the most forces stationed abroad, plus the greatest number of deliverable nuclear weapons. We also hold the world title for military spending, dropping as much cash as almost all other nations combined. We're home to the Salvation Army, the world's largest fund-raising charity. We produce the most nuclear and geothermal energy. We have the most Internet users. We spend the most money per person on health care every year. We have the world's most Nobel Prize winners. We have the biggest food, such as the world's largest burger (made by Mallie's Sports Bar & Grill in Southgate, Michigan; it weighs 134 pounds and spans two feet in diameter) and the world's tallest cookie tower (made by Girl Scouts).

Not surprisingly, we also coined the phrase, "Go big or go home."

I've had personal experience on both ends of the consumption spectrum. I grew up in the D.C. suburbs, where my parents promoted a way of life that emphasized leaving only the smallest of footprints. We'd leave the beat-up station wagon at home and schlep on public transportation into the city for all kinds of marches, rallies, and protests. The first time I was on TV was in third grade, angrily chanting about closing a leaking Texaco "tank farm." We made weekly trips to the recycling center. We belonged to a local food co-op, and would drive that old station wagon to a parking lot every Saturday morning to load up on sprouts, radishes, rutabaga, and other stuff we didn't quite know what to do with but tried in the name of being waste-avoiding locavores. We brought reusable tote bags everywhere so we never needed to use a new plastic bag. We spent our summer vacations camping, spitting biodegradable, all-natural toothpaste made out of calcium and apricot paste onto the ground, then using the edge of a sneaker to cover it over with dirt. We were vegetarians. We stocked the hippie staple Dr. Bronner's Magic All-One, a natural brew made from olive oil and peppermint extract, in every soap dispenser in the house, refilling old bottles with the stuff—to be used as mouthwash, shampoo, body wash, hand soap, dog shampoo, and dish soap. We were fighting the good fight. We were going the extra distance to live small, consume less, minimize our impact.

I carried that same torch through most of college. I did most of my clothes shopping in secondhand stores; I stayed vegetarian; I worked in an independent health food store; I volunteered at Food Not Bombs. I piled in a van with my friends and drove to Washington, D.C., for some environmental rally, standing for several hours in the incessant January rain, yelling through a bullhorn.

I remember asking my parents to meet us there, but they couldn't. They were going to my brother's basketball game, they said, and plus, it was so rainy.

Maybe they had just gotten too busy with work and school and activities and raking the leaves off the lawn. Maybe it was the pressure from my brother, who wouldn't tolerate the brown bread and sprouts sandwiches that had populated my reusable lunch bag for years. But when I came home from college one break, everything was different. The beat-up station wagon had been replaced with a red, shiny SUV. On the counter sat a loaf of Wonder bread, a departure from the nuts-and-seeds brown stuff we usually had from a local bakery. (Though it made for disappointing sandwiches, it made us feel good about choosing less-processed foods that as a result used less energy to produce.) The cabinets had a bag of trail mix with actual M&M's in it. Our organic wheaty munch cereal that tasted like Styrofoam was replaced with Kellogg's Frosted Flakes. The house smelled smoky and oily and weird.

"Was there a fire in here or something?" I said.

"Oh, I just made bacon for your brother this morning," my mom said. "But that was hours ago. I can't believe you can still smell it."

I looked around the house for my dad, expecting to see him in his normal position—hunched over the ancient computer, pecking out a letter of support or dissent to send to our congressperson. Instead, he was sitting on a brand-new leather couch, watching ESPN on the biggest television I'd ever seen not in a bar. We now had digital cable with hundreds of channels. My parents still wore tie-dye shirts, but now it seemed fake to me, a badge of honor they no longer deserved. That night, we went for dinner at my brother's favorite restaurant, the Outback Steakhouse, where the whole restaurant smelled of meat and the tables were arranged too far from the seats, as if they expected everyone to have a huge belly, which at this point, everyone in my family seemed to be developing.

I ordered mashed potatoes and then sulkily picked at them, complaining they tasted like beef, as if I had any idea what that might taste like.

I went back to school and rallied, volunteering more hours, chanting with more anger and passion and fight. I went vegan for a few weeks. I moved into a tiny, dumpy, drafty apartment in a run-down area of Pittsburgh where the sidewalks were dotted with smashed beer bottles, all because it made me feel grittier, smaller, closer to the source of . . . something. I persuaded myself that downsizing— not creating any new need for clothes from Indonesian sweatshops or for animals killed in slaughterhouses or anything mass-produced—was somehow living a more genuine life. By not having a car or a television, by purchasing used records instead of CDs, by getting my books from the library instead of the university's book center, by consuming as little as possible, I was minimizing the impact of my life. I admired my bike-riding friends who didn't own a car like all those lame polluters. I looked down on what was happening around my parents' suburban neighborhood, what I called "the Bigging": normal Colonial homes from the 1950s being plowed under for row after row of huge, generic McMansions, driveways filled with SUVs, people with more and more money to spend on making their lives bigger and bigger. I despised them and their bloated, easy lives. I never thought I'd be one of them.

But then, after college and embarking upon my grown-up life in Pittsburgh, Pennsylvania, I found myself, perhaps inevitably, falling right into it. It started easily enough, with my adoption of a (admittedly huge) dog, Ginsberg, a Saint Bernard. His snores resounded as though I'd let a bear cub into my house. When he'd give me a high five, his paw covered my palm. When I tried to get him into the bathtub, I could lift only one half of him at a time.

Strangers liked to remind me how big my dog was. If I was a little defensive about it, it was because, truthfully, Ginsberg was not the only oversized thing in my life.

There was my apartment, for starters—instead of saving money and living in a studio, or at least getting a roommate, I lived in a spacious town house. By myself. I claimed more space than I needed, and technically, more space than I could comfortably afford. In cities, space is the greatest luxury.

But I wasn't bothering anyone with my home. Why should I have been defensive about it? Maybe it's somewhere else I took up space—on the road. I had bought a Jeep Cherokee and used it often. I liked the big car because I could fit my big dog and all the big stuff I bought when I went to Target. (At the time I was also dating a guy who was six foot eight, but I chalk that up to coincidence.)

Maybe I was defensive out of a sense of guilt. Like everyone, I read the news; I knew about global warming and the war for oil; I knew driving an SUV instead of a hybrid wasn't helping these problems. Sometimes I shopped just because I was bored. I started buying my clothes at the Gap rather than at Goodwill because they didn't smell like lice-killer spray and they always came in my size. It became hard to retrace my steps. When had I stopped resisting the bigging of my own life?

It was easiest to blame the ones who couldn't defend themselves. First, the parents, a few hundred miles away. When they stopped resisting, started accumulating, letting their lives get bigger and easier, maybe it gave me some sort of tacit permission. I knew they wouldn't be disappointed with me if I also stopped fighting.

Or I could blame Ginsberg. Of course it's difficult to have a giant dog when you don't have a car—it just makes trips to obedience class and the vet and to the park on the other side of town that much more difficult. Deep down, though, I knew: I'd sold out. I'd taken yet another step to make my life easier, more convenient. Bigger. Instead of struggling myself, I was passing the struggle on to others, and making the problems of gas, oil, pollution, and waste bigger. But there was an uncomfortable truth motivating it all: big felt good.

I wound up living large the way many of us do—a little guilty, a little bewildered at how overblown my life had gotten, but also recognizing the real comfort in it. I thought about the distance between myself and the people who take big to the next level—worshipping in megachurches, driving Hummers, shopping at the Mall of America. To me, these people had lost all sense of scale, were living an extreme. Was I as far from them as I felt inside, as far as I hoped I was? Were they as bewildered and guilty and comfortable as I was with my big life, or had they come up with a way to feel better about it?

It was that question that motivated me to write this book, spending three years on the road, crisscrossing this country from New York to L.A. with stops all over in between. I learned that "big" looks different in small towns and major cities. It also wasn't nearly as black and white as I'd imagined. Yes, most things in America are bigger, and as we've all come to learn, bigger isn't always better—but it can be intriguing in surprising ways. Big America can be whimsical, as in the case of Francis Johnson, who spent his life winding the world's largest ball of twine, the only tourist attraction in Darwin, Minnesota. It can be alarming, as in the case of American women, who get the largest breast implants of women anywhere in the world.

Big America can indeed be easier or more efficient, like the largest landfill in the country, where scientists have learned to turn gas from our trash into clean power for thousands of L.A.-area homes. Even consuming big, from big-box chain stores, can be a salve, which I saw as an ill teen raked armfuls of electronics into his cart, his gift from the Make-A-Wish Foundation. The big money we sometimes spend buying stuff makes us feel better, if only temporarily. Most of us go big in some aspects of our lives, and what that means in America is as diverse as America itself—eclectic, powerful, progressive, quirky, stubborn, patriotic.

What follows is a ride—sometimes in a subcompact car, sometimes in a Hummer—into the heart of living large. I spent hundreds of hours experiencing some of the largest attractions in the country, conducting countless interviews with experts who come down on both sides of big, and real people who proudly defend it as their God-given right as Americans. I set out to learn about why living large is sometimes purposeful and obvious and in other cases unavoidable or even unbeknownst to us. This book is my attempt to witness firsthand the various ways our lives are supersized and to understand why expansion is part of our country's DNA. And when that meant eating at the world's largest pickle bar, you can bet I stepped up.

I.

THE McMANSION EXPANSION

Kathy, a longtime friend from Northern Virginia, invited me over to her Manhattan apartment. She said she wanted to share some big news. As I walked the familiar sixteen blocks from my place to hers, I thought about what the news could be. Within the last year, she'd gotten married and she and her husband were about to have a baby. They lived in—by New York standards—a fancy-schmancy place, since the building was three blocks from the subway and had an elevator, a gym, a terrace, and a doorman. As soon as she swung open her door, she laid it on me: they were moving. Back to the D.C. suburbs, into a big new house. With all of the baby accoutrements (the crib, stroller, jogging stroller, carrier, and changing table all gathered in a corner, waiting), it was true that their once-spacious apartment felt stuffed. I was sad for her to leave the city—and me—but I knew the move, back to her family and to a home with lots of room for her new family to grow, was a great one for her. A few months later, they were gone.

Once they'd gotten settled, Kathy invited me to come see the house and, of course, the adorable baby, who was crawling by then. They'd set up in a community in Montgomery County, Maryland, what's been called "the heart of mansion country."

To get there, I drove past 8,000-square-foot house after house, set along what used to be rolling pastures of horse country. These days, it's one of the wealthiest counties in America, and has the country's largest percentage of residents older than twenty-five years old who hold a postgraduate degree (nearly a third of the residents).

What makes a house a McMansion?—defined as "a modern house built on a large and imposing scale, but regarded as ostentatious and lacking architectural integrity." These fit the mold: brand-new, grandiose cookie-cutter architecture, very large, and in this case built on a lot that once contained a smaller house. Driving around the bucolic-sounding, sweetly named streets (Quince Orchard Road, Chestnut Hill Street, even a Placid Street), it felt like I'd fallen into Candyland, with identical gingerbread houses lining every identical street. There were no yards to speak of, since the lots were mostly a quarter of an acre, with a matter of just a few feet separating the windows of neighbors' living rooms. The neighborhood contains 1,800 homes. In the mid-'90s, Walmart actually proposed setting up a 160,000-square-foot store in the middle of the neighborhood, though the plan ultimately fizzled.

I was struck by the sheer *size* of the houses. They were as garish as a row of gold teeth. And Kathy had definitely moved into a McMansion. Most homes in the neighborhood were larger than 5,000 square feet, which just about doubles the national average. In classic McMansion form, the houses looked pristine from the street, but the other three sides were done as inexpensively as possible; the curb appeal of brick was replaced with miles of white vinyl siding. Houses were a mishmash of overly ornate styles, what *Slate* architecture critic Witold Rybczynski rounds up as "architectural bits and pieces: a portico, classical columns, Palladian [rounded at the top] windows, dentil [small rectangular blocks] moldings at the eaves, even quoins [stone trim at the corners]. They all add up to—what? No style that I can identify, like a badly mismatched outfit . . . producing a caricature. It isn't just that [McMansions] are big, like their namesake Big Macs; it's that they celebrate bigness." Out of all the places in the world, why would Kathy—cosmopolitan, bright, tasteful Kathy—want to live here?

John Stilgoe, professor of the history of landscape at Harvard University, tells me that though he would never choose to live in a McMansion—also called a Garage Mahal, Starter Castle, or Hummer House—he sees the appeal.

"McMansions are mostly practical," he argues. "A house that big allows you to get away from your family and have private personal space, whereas a small apartment would not."

I think back to the loads of baby supplies piled in Kathy's old apartment. In her case, upsizing not only made sense; it seemed downright mandatory.

"It's practical because you can have an attic where you store things like old dining-room sets. Then when the kids are grown up and furnishing their first place, you don't have to run out and buy everything new, since you had room to store things," he says.

I mention that there are lots of homes with attics and basements that aren't McMansions.

"It's also a way for people to show their status and wealth," he says. "Some people do it through fancy benefits, some with clothes, and some do it with houses. I feel sorry for them, thinking they have something to prove or that they have to put it right out there to get validation."

The supersized house as a supersized way to show off. It sounds

obvious. But that doesn't sound like Kathy, either. So what else is
it that could motivate someone to buy big?

"The American house has been swelling for decades," said a 2002
article in *The New York Times*. "It has swollen even though it
stands on a smaller lot. It has swollen even though a smaller family
lives in it." Since 1940, the average number of people living in an
American home has dropped from 3.7 to 2.6, but the average size
of new houses has grown. The average American home ballooned
from 983 square feet in 1950 to 2,349 square feet in 2004, a 140
percent increase in size. Homes are then landscaped to look even
larger, with many buyers requesting fewer trees and less vegeta-
tion to bring less attention to the land and more to the house.

The neighborhoods where Kathy and I grew up, in the D.C.
suburbs of Northern Virginia, consisted mostly of houses built in
the 1950s and '60s. They were a mix of different styles, some with
flat roofs, or bricks covered in ivy, or classic Colonials, each set on
a one-acre lot with a tree-filled backyard. I noticed, though, every
time I went home to visit that a swath of woods surrounding my
neighborhood was being bulldozed, rows of identical McMansions
popping up in its place. I thought I was imagining, or at least ex-
aggerating the trend, until I read that five of the nation's ten top
big-house communities are in the D.C. suburbs—and of those, in
such communities as Fairfax and Montgomery County, Maryland,
more than two-thirds of the houses have nine rooms or more, not
counting bathrooms or utility rooms. And it's not just going on
around Washington, D.C.—other places around the country are
becoming known for McMansion sprawl, including the suburbs of
Chicago, Denver, Salt Lake City, Minneapolis, Philadelphia, Austin,

Santa Fe, Los Angeles, and Atlanta. About two-thirds of the country's largest cities have McMansions.

In 2007, the average size of a new house in America hit a record 2,302 square feet. According to *Realtor* magazine, we'd been growing for a long time. In the 1920s, middle-class homes "were essentially two rooms wide by three-four rooms deep." Despite the baby boom in the early 1950s, the average middle-class home stayed around the same size but due to the new ranch-style, was just rotated to "three-four rooms wide by two rooms deep." Our families weren't getting any bigger, but by the greed-is-good 1980s, the modest family-style ranch home was out of vogue, and the McMansion was born. As homes were built farther away from city cores, developers began to crowd two-story homes on smaller lots. Imposing facades became more important to home buyers than backyard barbecues.

Kathy takes me through the sprawling foyer, a vision in beige. The new carpet is beige. The walls are beige. Even though she has a few pieces of beautiful framed art hanging up, the walls are so expansive that they still feel bare. We walk through a living room, an office, a dining room, another living space, and the massive kitchen. We head upstairs to more rooms, more beige walls with cathedral ceilings, and more beige carpeting. For all of the architectural mishmash outside, McMansions are nothing if not uniform inside. She shows me the palatial master bedroom. Even with a massively fluffy bed in the center, the room still seems empty. The *New York Times* article said that most New York apartments could fit in the bedroom of a McMansion, and that holds true for Kathy's old apartment and new bedroom. Though she's been in the house for a few months and made several expensive trips to Pottery Barn, the house still feels unlived-in. Maybe that's because in a house this large, with two adults and an infant, it's impossible to use even half of this space.

We head downstairs to the finished basement, again beige. I'm getting unnerved by the uniformity of it all. It's not that Kathy has a fetish for bland—quite the opposite. She dresses with polish and sophistication and always has the baby decked out in adorably hip kid gear. This is simply the way of McMansions, and my fashionable friend Kathy's is no exception: it's generic, standard-issue, inoffensive. The basement is divided evenly between a playroom for baby and a playroom for daddy. The grown-ups' side has a massive flat-screen TV and deep leather couches. The baby's side looks like a Toys "R" Us, with every kind of action hero and toy car and gray-matter-building games and stuffed animal strewn across the floor. Despite all of the furniture and mounds of kid stuff, the room still feels cavernous and empty. Though the old adage is that home is where you hang your hat or where the heart is, I can't imagine ever feeling at home in such an uncozy, looming structure. As we climb the steps to go back upstairs and Kathy excitedly tells me about a new chair, I think of the line about McMansions from co-median Mo Rocca: "Who among us has walked through a 'Great Room' and not expected to meet the Bachelor waiting with a rose?" It's apropos because this house feels about as authentic as reality TV.

The home is the most personal place in the world. It's no wonder that the house is the cornerstone of the American dream. Buying a bigger home is an unparalleled form of expression—a tangible way to show yourself and everyone else—that you're movin' on up. It makes sense that so many of us would want a marker for what we've achieved. So who cares if someone wants to live in a McMansion?

Critics say the influx of McMansions affects not just its occupants, but the entire community around them. Tearing down houses to build supersized ones in their place puts stress on older infrastructure. The good news is that McMansions can send property values soaring; the bad news is that, as a result, tax rates also soar, which can force out longtime residents.

Building any new home, rather than moving into a home that already exists, creates a demand for new materials. It consumes huge resources: the lumber used for a typical 3,000-square-foot house stretched end to end would exceed four miles. Americans broke wood consumption records in 2004 and again in 2005, according to the Western Wood Products Association, to frame more than two million new houses in the latter year. "A house will spend decades cranking out carbon dioxide and other greenhouse gases. Over a fifty-year lifetime, greenhouse emissions caused by the standard American house account for thirty to forty times the weight of the carbon that's socked away in its wood frame. The bigger the house, the bigger the emissions," writes Stan Cox in an article called "Big Houses Are Not Green: America's McMansion Problem."

To assuage Americans' enviroguilt, many builders are offering to construct "green" supersized houses. That's an oxymoron. "A 1,500-square-foot house with mediocre energy-performance standards will use far less energy for heating and cooling than a 3,000-square-foot house of comparable geometry with much better energy detailing," said a 2005 report in the *Journal of Industrial Ecology*. "Additional energy is wasted by the longer heating/cooling ducts and hot-water pipes in a big house," notes Cox, "and such houses have more surface area, thus requiring more fossil fuel to cool and heat them." So even if someone builds a McMansion with energy-saving materials, the impact is, at best, equivalent to that of a smaller house, but certainly isn't a net plus to the environment.

Some areas—including Atlanta, Austin, Los Angeles, and Montgomery County, Maryland—have begun instituting rules about the maximum height of new homes and, in some cases, design approval boards to try to control supersize sprawl. Wood-Ridge, New Jersey, said a home couldn't take up more than 55 percent of its lot, while in Arlington County, Virginia, an even stricter rule was passed: a home's footprint can take up no more than 30 percent of its lot.

With ever-falling mortgage rates, a climate that considered real estate a sound investment, and an anybody-gets-a-loan credit situation, it's no wonder McMansions became the suburban status quo. In 2003, Jonathan Clements wrote an article for *The Wall Street Journal* called "The Problem Is the Big House, Not the Small Salary," where he compared home costs. "Newly constructed single-family homes had a median size of 2,114 square feet in 2002, up from 1,520 square feet in 1982. That's a 39 percent increase in twenty years," he wrote. After crunching numbers, he figured that getting that larger 2,114-square-foot house would only cost $281 more a month than the 1,520-square-foot house, which makes it astonishingly clear why so many middle-class families were able to stretch their way into McMansions. "Even as homes have ballooned in size, interest rates have tumbled," wrote Clements. "Thanks to twenty years of falling mortgage rates, today's buyers are getting more house for less money. It almost seems too good to be true. And, of course, it is too good to be true."

During the lending free-for-all, McMansions didn't seem like an unwise investment. But after the housing market took a violent downturn, many were trapped in their McMansion decision; by 2009, one in eight of all homeowners faced foreclosure. Take, for example, Loudon County, Virginia, another D.C. suburb, that often boasts the country's highest median income, about $107,207. It's roughly about fifteen miles from where Kathy lives. "At the end of 2007, twenty of the twenty-five houses for sale for more than $850,000 in Loudoun County appeared to be foreclosures," said a 2008 Reuters article. "One out of every sixty-nine households in the county was in foreclosure, well above the national average of one filing for every 555 households." Wealthy—or aspirational— families signed up for loans during boom times, but during bust, McMansions became nearly impossible to pay for—or unload. "These can take years to sell, as they must compete with brand-new developments still coming online . . . there's no market for a million-dollar rental property."

McMansion foreclosures hurt more than the people who put their names on the mortgages, and more than the investors who got caught in the downturn. A 2008 article in *The Atlantic* pointed out that "the crisis is harming the neighbors of people in foreclosure, even those who aren't having trouble making loan payments . . . every foreclosure reduces the value of all other houses within an eighth of a mile by about 1 percent, as the sight of vacant property scares off potential buyers. Combine that with a market already in decline, and neighborhoods that begin to have troubles can go off the cliff." The article lists areas "with at least a veneer of affluence" that have been especially hard-hit, including the suburbs surrounding Las Vegas, Miami-Dade County, California's Central Valley, much of Florida and the Southwest, eastern Colorado, and Greater Atlanta.

A few related factors make McMansions less and less appealing every day. The first is obvious: the recession, and belt-tightening, make them impractical at best, impossible at worst. The second is the spike in home heating and cooling costs, which makes tightening the belt even less realistic for McMansion dwellers (a *Wall Street Journal* example figured it can cost $5,000 a year or more to heat and cool a 5,000-square-foot house in a city such as Farmington, Connecticut). The third is that many of the 78 million baby boomers who voraciously acquired supersized houses in the '90s through the mid-'00s are aging out. As boomers become empty nesters and look to retire on ever-shrinking 401(k)s, many are attempting to sell their McMansions and downsize to smaller, more affordable living spaces. Add to that all of the foreclosed McMansions already on the market, and we're left with a glut of houses that are expensive to heat and cool and often require at least half-hour commutes. Many McMansion owners bought high (home prices peaked mid-2006) and would have no option but to sell low, since home prices have since plummeted in record numbers. According to the Standard & Poor's/Case-Shiller home price index, in October 2008, home prices were down 18 percent from just a year earlier, the sharpest decline in the data's two-decade history; they'd fallen a whopping 23.4 percent since the mid-2006 peak. Some McMansion hubs, including Phoenix, Las Vegas, and San Francisco, all faced 30 percent or more declines in value, making all homes—but especially supersized ones—a burden to unload. Even without a degree in economics, it's clear to me that high supply and low demand aren't a winning category for housing.

In addition, the houses (often built with less durable materials and less sturdy construction) are at least a decade old and in need of maintenance. As a 2008 article by Christopher B. Leinberger, a professor of urban planning at the University of Michigan, notes, "High-end McMansions are cheaply built. Hollow doors and wallboard are less durable than solid-oak doors and lath-and-plaster walls. The plywood floors that lurk under wood veneers or carpeting tend to break up and warp as the glue that holds the wood together dries out; asphalt-shingle roofs typically need replacing after ten years. Many recently built houses take what structural integrity they have from drywall—their thin wooden frames are too flimsy to hold the houses up."

Home, sweet home!

Part of the reason the future looks so bleak for McMansions has to do with the regulations surrounding them. Subdividing the giant houses into living spaces for more than one family, a sensible option, is forbidden by many local jurisdictions, who keep laws on the book that don't allow nonrelated people to share a house. The rules are often a misguided attempt to clamp down on immigrants and the less affluent—a way to limit a high-end neighborhood to just those who can afford it.

Without anyone to move into these vacant McMansions, I wouldn't be the first to imagine the country's suburbs as tomorrow's version of Western ghost towns, tumbleweeds blowing by ornate French doors. Arthur C. Nelson, director of the Metropolitan Institute at Virginia Tech, predicts that by 2025, about 40 percent, of about 22 million, of today's large-lot houses will be surplus. Leinberger even predicts that "Many low-density suburbs and McMansion subdivisions, including some that are lovely and affluent today, may become what inner cities became in the 1960s and '70s—slums characterized by poverty, crime, and decay."

* * *

It isn't a stretch to say that McMansions are bad for the environment, bad for aesthetics, and bad financial investments. And Americans wouldn't have indulged in them so heavily if they weren't able to get their hands on mortgages (and get in over their heads) thanks to subprime lenders. But none of that answers the most important question: why did we want McMansions so badly in the first place?

Robert Frank, a professor of economics at Cornell University, doesn't buy the notion that a big house is just a way to announce your status from the (turreted) rooftops.

"I think most people don't experience what they're doing as 'keeping up with the Joneses,'" he said. "The people in the middle are not looking at the wealthy and saying, 'Oh, we've got to have that'; they don't think in those terms. They just see mansions and think, *That's fun, maybe someday my kids will have a place like that.* But it's not like they're angry or envious or trying to emulate the wealthy."

Then how did so many of us end up clamoring for McMansions?

"It's just one step at a time," Frank explains. "You're more affected by your context. Instead of asking ourselves, 'What are the richest people doing?' it's really more like, 'What do people like me do around here?' It's been a race to keep up that has been very, very difficult for families in the middle because if you don't participate in that, if you don't match the spending on housing of other people at your income level, the rub is that your kids are going to go to below-average schools.

"The modern family in the middle faces the choice between saving enough for retirement and sending their kids to unsafe schools with low test scores or taking all their money out of savings and scraping together a down payment on a house in a better school district. They have chosen option two," he said.

It is, in its way, an encouraging notion. It isn't sheer greed or conspicuous consumption motivating the supersizing. Instead, it's a way to access the *real* American dream for your kids, to give them a better education, the chance at a better life than the generation before them. Frank's theory also helps account for why so many middle-class Americans were willing to mortgage it all—literally—to get their families into larger homes (this wasn't as prevalent in the past, he explains, because it wasn't possible; you had to put down 25 to 30 percent on a house, whereas the '00s introduced no-money-down homes).

Kathy's decision to move into a McMansion neighborhood makes infinitely more sense through this lens and goes a long way toward explaining her decision. She's not trying to show off, or rub her wealth in the face of others. On the contrary: she's got a new baby now, and she's already thinking about the best public kindergarten. Whether her move, echoed by millions of other families, remains the norm for upwardly mobile families depends heavily on the shape of the economy and, moreover, our willingness to reverse a course that has already caused untold damage to our environment, economy, finances, and neighborhoods.

What will the future hold for the American dream house? After we recover from our record foreclosures, will we rebuild more sensibly, or start supersizing again? John Stilgoe of Harvard thinks that, for all our best green intentions, big cars and big houses aren't going anywhere.

"My students are stymied nowadays. They believe in sustainability and talk about being green," he says. "They'd be embarrassed to drive an SUV like many of their parents do; instead, they want a Prius. But in terms of housing, they—especially the women—don't want to have smaller closets, or fewer clothes to put in them. My students" (ostensibly some of the brightest young minds in the country) "are dulled by the collision of the way of thinking we had through 2007 and the situation we actually face today."

2.

INSIDE THE MEGACHURCH

Though the North Way Christian Community Church was built in the 1990s, it looks '60s or '70s retro, with a nearly flat roof painted a soft light blue. The only way you'd know it was a church, as opposed to a library or a rec center, is the giant steeple emerging from the flatness. Trees surround the building and its parking lot. Cement walls and pillars, which give the idea of ancient sandstone, hold up the roof. It's right off Perry Highway, in the suburbs of Pittsburgh, Pennsylvania. It's been here, in a town called Wexford, since 1994, growing every year. Other than its unconventional design, you might assume it was just like any other church.

People shut their car doors behind them and approach the building, wearing panty hose and sensible shoes or jeans and skateboarding sneakers and Hawaiian shirts. A few signs along the weaving road that leads to the parking lot say: NEW TO OUR CHURCH? TURN YOUR RADIO TO 88.7. In the spring sun, several people mill around the outside of the big glass doors, chatting and sipping from little plastic cups of lemonade. North Way is a megachurch; it has about three thousand people coming to services every weekend.

"Over the years, it's just grown," says North Way's Pastor Jay. "We never set out to be this big. We didn't put a target on the wall saying we want to be three thousand people or anything. Yeah, we're big enough to qualify as a megachurch now, but I think that is just the result of providing a quality experience for people." North Way, like most megachurches, doesn't do any advertising, and relies on its parishioners' word of mouth to recruit new worshippers. And the strategy works—roughly 80 percent of megachurchgoers say they came because they were personally invited there by a friend, family member, or coworker. According to research by Dave Travis, coauthor of *Beyond Megachurch Myths: What We Can Learn From America's Largest Churches,* worshippers at small churches have invited an average of one person to their church that year; for megachurch worshippers, that number is five.

So odds are, I'm probably not the only first-timer here at North Way today. According to a 2008 article in *The New York Times,* "evangelical churches around the country have enjoyed steady growth over the last decade," meaning lots of new members. Some other churches are also growing; the article notes that "some large Roman Catholic parishes and mainline Protestant churches around the nation indicated attendance increases, too. But they were nowhere near as striking as those reported by congregations describing themselves as evangelical, a term generally applied to churches that stress the literal authority of Scripture and the importance of personal conversion, or being 'born again.'" The article went on to say that, in particular, "Bad times are good for evangelical churches."

I'm here because North Way (both big and evangelical) is simultaneously conservative and progressive. This church offers its weekly sermon via podcast, so you can download it to your iPod and listen to it anywhere. I'd heard they have live music. I'd read that they run a Web site with a Jesus-themed blog. I wonder how they could make a several-thousand-member congregation, one of the main factors that qualifies North Way as a megachurch, feel like "a really small church with lots of people!" as testimonials on their Web site advertise. They also quote people saying, "I never knew church could be so fun!" That some folks think church is fun doesn't surprise or interest me so much. What does intrigue me is a church that *advertises* itself as fun, a church with several thousand members that prides itself on feeling small and intimate.

A criticism of megachurches is that they draw members away from smaller churches, but there is certainly no shortage of traditional places to worship—right now, megachurches represent only about 1 percent of all churches in America. Though we didn't invent the megachurch (London's Baptist Metropolitan Tabernacle had five thousand members in the late 1800s), we've popularized it. In 1970, there were just ten in America. In 1990, 250 fit that description.

Today, there are roughly 1,900 megachurches, where millions of people worship on any given Sunday. Some estimates say that a new megachurch emerges in the United States every two days. So what are these three million people telling us about how America wants to worship now?

I'm wondering what megachurch members are looking for, and whether it's the same thing as members of traditional churches. I'm still a beginner on the journey toward spiritual life—I don't know where I'm going, or where I might end up. I'm also not sure I'll ever be someone who gets on board with organized religion. I can't even get myself to join a running club or writers' association; I'm just not much of a joiner. Growing up, my family was Reform Jewish, but almost secular—we were more into noshing on bagels than reading the Torah. Still, for all the big holidays, we attended services and hosted a dining room full of relatives. My parents liked feeling connected to a community, going into synagogue and shaking hands and hugging the same people. My mom always said she liked being tied into the traditions of religion, thousands of years of the same celebrations, prayers, and recipes. It's a sentiment I've heard again and again from friends and family of various religions, taking comfort and strength in relying on both the routines and the community.

Places like North Way seem to offer something different. If a church has several thousand members, how can you possibly feel closely connected? Is it even more comforting to have your beliefs affirmed by so many like-minded members? Does praying with thousands make your voice feel stronger, or does it get lost among the others?

No one at North Way knows, as far as I can tell, that I'm not a regular member. At a megachurch (commonly defined as any non-Catholic church with at least two thousand members for weekly services), they're always looking for new members, so there's a great emphasis on friendliness and inclusiveness. Hired professional musicians are common, playing pop-styled music. They use amplification and PA systems. Hymns are projected on screens, so they often don't use hymnals or Bibles. A recent study showed that 90 percent of megachurches use projection equipment for every single service. Movie theater–style chairs are the norm. Most feature a charismatic, authoritative senior minister (nationally, 89 percent of them are white) and a "very active, seven-day-a-week congregational community." The focus on entertainment leads some critics to call them McChurches or Disney Churches. North

Way, which feels so new and unique to me, is just one of eight megachurches in this state. Though Nevada and Rhode Island are tied for the least with one each, every state in America has a megachurch.

When I walk in the front doors, my eyes land on the bookstore/gift shop. It's stocked with pumpkin-scented candles and racks of books on God. Dave Travis's research shows that a coffee shop is the most popular "extra" for a megachurch, closely followed by a bookstore. "The suburban megachurch campus has more of a mall-like feel," he says. Travis explains that these in-church businesses are set up based on sociologist Ray Oldenburg's "third place" theory: if you are defined by where you spend your time, you have your first place (for example, home) and a second place (probably work), but your third place is up for grabs—the gym, your bar hangout, the place you take night classes. With enticing extras where you can spend even more time, the megachurch is vying to be your third place.

Outside the bookshop, the lobby is a flurry of bodies, like an airport. It's got helpful kiosks. The ceilings are domed and glorious, like being inside a snow globe (how this effect is achieved, considering the flat roof I saw from the outside, is beyond me). Everyone's wearing printed name tags, like the woman's that reads: KAREN T., BEECHVIEW, with a green cartoon tree next to the name. The name tags come from a wall across from the bathroom, row after row of preprinted name tags to peel and stick onto your shirt for all of the members. Two greeters, who stand inside the main glass entrance doors, shake hands and introduce themselves to strangers as if they're welcoming longtime friends into their own home, all hugs and "Good to see yas!" Jimmy and Carol, a couple who've been at this church for three years since moving from St. Louis, want me to ask them if I have any questions. Though of course they are friendly, they're almost aggressively so, the same way store greeters can make you feel pressured to buy something or at least enlist their help, even when you don't want it. A heavy lady in a pink turtleneck tells me I look lost and says that the young people usually sit to the left. I hear the sounds of bustle and talking and shopping and singing coming from farther inside. My eyes dart around, trying to find a focus point in all of the people and music, a sensory overload.

In a survey of more than a thousand regular megachurch attendees, only 51 percent could say that "personal prayer was emphasized a lot." Smaller groups within the church are set up to offer the tight-knit feeling of personal, intimate support. At North Way, there are groups for families, singles in their twenties, thirties, and forties, seniors, couples, mothers of preschoolers, middle school students, high school students, and special interest groups, like hikers. There are two hundred small groups in all, made up of about ten to twelve people each, which meet once a week in a member's home. Like strip malls or big-box stores, this megachurch seems to be offering everything in one place—and that's apparently one of its best selling points.

"We can offer much more specific ministry opportunities," says North Way's Pastor Jay. "For example, we have a divorce recovery ministry with a full counseling center on our campus and fourteen therapists available. We've got children's ministries, junior high and high school ministries all on our campus. So a large church can offer many different ministries that a smaller church just doesn't have the resources to offer, and that can be very attractive, from child care all the way to adult training."

And though critics might compare megachurches to cities, in that people are alone together, "anonymity is definitely an attracting factor," says Pastor Jay. "I've been to some smaller churches where they have you raise your hand if you're new. Some people don't want to be known as a visitor. They just want to come explore or they're just checking it out, and a larger church allows for complete anonymity. You can come for weeks, and just slide in and slide out until you're ready to have someone know you're there, to get engaged. You decide when you want to let that be known. It's up to you to set the pace of your involvement."

When someone does decide to keep attending the church, he usually joins a small group. "That way when you come into church, you say, 'Hey, there's two people from my small group,' and you'll sit together," says Pastor Jay. "All of a sudden you're not just one person lost in this huge crowd. I usually say that in six months, if you do not become a member and join a small group, you'll start to feel like this isn't your church home." That said, nonjoiners are in the minority. "About 80 percent of our people are in small groups," he says.

Those groups are one way of making a massive cross-section of people feel more like a tight-knit community. But people don't necessarily need that, argues Travis, because we've become so accustomed to big that we're not put off by it anymore.

"This country has experienced a growth in scale of every major public institution," he says. He gives a personal example from suburban Atlanta, Georgia: "In 1954, my parents finished high school with a graduating class of 150. Twenty-five years later, I graduated with 255 kids. My daughter graduated in 2009 with more than a thousand kids. The definition of large has changed." It's a similar story where I grew up, and in lots of suburbs around the country. "I also see it in our houses—I grew up in a house, a nice home in a nice community, and it was 1,400 square feet. Twenty years later, when my wife and I were buying our first home, a nice house was 2,500 square feet. Our sense of what's a normal size has expanded. Big universities are growing the same way, and if you attended a college with 30,000 students, going to a megachurch with 3,700 people isn't going to seem that overwhelming. Basically, my contention is that as people become socialized into larger and larger institutions, the megachurch doesn't seem so weird anymore."

As I step inside the sanctuary, the music blasts. People sway, the crowd dotted with men holding their hands in the air, doing a slow, unself-conscious wave. A stage spans the width of the room. Red velvet curtains are parted to bookend the source of the music: a choir of twenty-five plain-clothed parishioners, four microphoned singers being led by a bald singer in a black suit and a salmon-colored T-shirt. To stage right are people playing a piano, an organ, acoustic guitars, basses, clarinets, trumpets, and trombones. There's a percussion section with a full drum set that's encased in Plexiglas, plus a man who's patting African drums. The music is highly orchestrated and sounds concert-quality, and the mix of strain and joy on the performers' faces makes it clear that this means the world to them.

"To only a God like you, do I give my praise," sing nearly all of the people I pass as I file to my seat. There are no Bibles provided, nothing on the smooth backs of the seats. Now they sing the chorus, "Only a God like you, only a God like you." The lyrics are projected on gigantic, six-by-eight-foot projection screens, one on either side of the stage and one on the rear wall, likely for the performers. Behind the lyrics are pink, yellow, and purple psychedelic swirling patterns. The image behind the words changes to a crucifix on a grassy hill, a reminder that this isn't just a soft rock concert.

David F. Wells, a megachurch critic who has been ordained since 1965, studies church and culture as a professor at Massachusetts's Gordon-Conwell Theological Seminary. "Evangelical churches should be the places where we find an alternative way of thinking about our world and living in it, one which in its profundity is a reflection of the God who is incomparable, not a threadbare mimicry of the culture," he says. Wells asserts that a crucial problem with megachurches is that they cater too much to what's comfortable for the individual, while they should have parishioners "asking not what the church can do for us, but what we can do for Christ in the church and in our broken world," that true evangelical churches should be "all about substance, not style." Those stylistic markers of a megachurch are exactly what offend Wells. He cites churches where the pastors ask themselves: "Do we have the latest technology? Is our screen big enough? Do we meet at times which don't get in the way of people enjoying their weekend? Have we eliminated all the things that offend them, like pulpits, crosses, hymnbooks, and pews? Do people leave the church feeling happy like they do when they go back to their hotel rooms from Disneyland?" Wells may be hyperbolic in his comparison of megachurches to Disneyland, but the underlying similarity of enjoyment and convenience adds to its validity. He explains that, "The temptation the church always experiences is to be like the world.

However, if the church is to be truly successful, it must be unlike anything else we find in life"—not celebrity pastors or pop music or gift shops that sell pumpkin-scented candles.

But as existing megachurches grow and new ones open, isn't that a mark of success, of reaching Christians? "A Christian faith that mutes its truth in order to fit in, and dilutes the commitment it asks for in order not to be off-putting, is doomed," Wells says. "The issue here is not traditional versus contemporary. The issue is authentic versus inauthentic." He suggests that not only should churches not bend to popular culture, but that they should offer a 180-degree opposition to pop culture. "Surely, in what we think and do, in the way we live and act, we should be expressing what the alternative is to our increasingly paganized culture," he says.

When the song "Only a God Like You" is over, I plop down in the chair. It's not austere, molded plastic like the ones I endured for a decade of Jewish services. It's not stoic, firm, or communal, like the pews at my friends' weddings at Catholic churches. Instead, it's plush and padded, exactly like a seat in a movie theater or a stadium, only without the jumbo cup holder. But the chairs aren't just for backside comfort—they're for emotional comfort.

"As we've expanded elsewhere, so has our idea of what constitutes safe personal space," says Travis. "Thirty years ago, people didn't mind packing into church, but now we want just a little bit more space between us and the next guy. That's the appeal of this type of seating—even if it's unconscious, you feel you have more personal space from the stranger next to you than you would on a pew."

He says the chairs are carefully designed by architects to make worshippers feel like there are *more* people at church. An average megachurch runs five or six services every weekend. Half of those are completely packed, with every seat taken. The other services aren't at full capacity, which can make worshippers feel uncomfortable or even view it as a lack of validation for their decision to attend that church.

"In the same way people don't want to feel too cramped, they also don't want to feel too spread out. You don't want to be in a room that's only 10 percent full," says Travis. "So church architects and interior designers have found that if all the seats are the same color, you can tell that there are lots of empty seats. But if you have three or four different color chairs that you vary in a certain pattern, your eye can't tell the capacity at a quick glance. That makes it feel more full, even when only 50 or 60 percent of the seats are actually taken. It makes you think there are a lot of other people here today, too."

Megachurches are big money—last year's average income per church was $6 million. That's perhaps because many megachurches focus on fundraising. Also, megachurch worshippers tend to give more to their churches than people who attend smaller churches (a lot of this could be due to socioeconomic factors, since most megachurches are in suburban areas, where there tends to be a high per capita income to begin with). Not surprisingly, businesses are sprouting up to help churches turn into megachurches and turn megachurches into mega-megachurches. Right now, the largest church in America is Lakewood Church in Houston, Texas, with 25,060 members. It holds services in the former Houston Rockets' stadium, where, one could argue, people have been praying for a long time. Close behind is the World Changers Church in College Park, Georgia, with 23,093 members; of the country's five largest churches, three of them are in Texas—and two of those are in Houston. It seems every church wants to grow, and to use that growth as a sign that its believers must be on to something good.

A recent book called *PastorPreneur,* by John Jackson, which is sold in Christian bookstores, encourages church leaders to think and act like business entrepreneurs. Kingdom Ventures is a company whose mission is to help churches expand, and has worked with more than 10,000 churches so far. Many megachurches have been criticized for adopting traditional business models, like those of Walmart, including "intensive market research, heavy reliance upon opinion polls, and polished advertising targeted at affluent young professionals," according to an article in *BusinessWeek.*

Here we are, worshipping at the Church of Stuff. We're still being marketed to, persuaded to buy here rather than there. The *BusinessWeek* article went on to point out the in-church cafés and coffee shops that are supposed to feel like Starbucks, the bookstores, and nail salons. This year, the 16.4-million-member Southern Baptist Convention plans to "plant" 1,800 new churches using traditional MBA-style niche-marketing tactics. "We have cowboy churches for people working on ranches, country music churches, even several motorcycle churches aimed at bikers," says their spokesman.

It makes sense that churches are trying to woo worshippers. After all, even large denominations like the United Methodist Church and the Episcopal Church have been shrinking for decades, losing a total of more than a million members in the past several years. When the recession hit in 2008, millions of Americans watched their years of hard work crumble, their 401(k)s tank, and their homes foreclose. That's a call to faith if there ever was one. But the percentage of Americans attending religious services didn't budge. It may be surprising, but both the Pew Forum on Religion and Public Life and a Gallup Poll showed that more people weren't going to services. The surveys measure only actual attendance, not religiosity, so it's possible the financial crisis caused more people to turn to religion at home, maybe praying there more often or saying grace before meals. Still, it's surprising that 39 percent of Americans reported attending worship service at least weekly as of January 2009—the exact same percentage of attendees as in January 2007, when the Dow was nearly twice as high. So it makes sense that churches would do whatever they could do to bring in new customers. Joel Osteen, pastor of Houston's Lakewood megachurch (the one that holds services in the former Rockets' stadium), has seen contributions from his church reach $55 million in a single year. "Other churches have not kept up," he says, "and they lose people by not changing with the times."

The hottest trend in megachurches is not just expanding across one giant campus, but setting up "multisites," or many smaller campuses around the area. That way, they can cater to the specific population—suburban parents or college students, for example. "The biggest challenge is undoubtedly the age gap. A sixty-five-year-old is not going to like the same music that a twenty-five-year-old likes," says Pastor Jay. "That's why North Way is moving toward multisite campusing." Its honed approach to appealing to members is similar to what megachurches do with their "there's one for everyone!" small groups.

Some megachurches are even franchising their names, like Oklahoma's Life Church, which has expanded to six campuses in different states, doing market research to decide where to open next.

Others offer the sort of pitch you'd expect from a TV commercial. The audacious Creflo A. Dollar, pastor of World Changers Church International in College Park, Georgia, promises "prosperity" if you believe, and he doesn't mean it just in terms of how your soul will fare in the afterlife. Dollar drives a Rolls-Royce, keeps another one in his garage, and travels in his own Gulfstream jet. When your pastor lives like that, you don't have to feel guilty about the stuff you've collected, or for valuing stuff in the first place, or for wanting to obtain more stuff. It's a big departure from the often-quoted, "It is easier for a camel to go through the eye of a needle than for a rich man to enter the kingdom of God."

I wonder about the shift to accommodation and entertainment. Many of the megachurches advertise themselves as nondenominational so they can attract as many members as possible. This from institutions that seemed inflexible almost by their nature. You as the individual had to make concessions in order to do what your church wanted—showing up at the same time every Sunday, dressing up, keeping your teen from dyeing her hair some wacky Crayola color, enduring the uncomfortable seats. But with megachurches, it's the opposite; they cater to the public by delivering the secular, not in message, but in form. The religious message of megachurches may not be a departure, but how they deliver it, and the traditions they're willing to forego to increase membership, have changed dramatically.

We all know the ugly stereotype about Americans, that we value convenience above all else. We want a church to serve us, not us having to serve the church. I can't think of a time in my experience when I felt like my religion was trying its best to court and satisfy me, finding out what I wanted and tailor-making itself to fit.

Nor can I imagine this going on in any other country. At North Way, they've got that *Price Is Right* "come on down!" mentality, no matter what you're wearing. Would Buddhists in Tibet add a brass band to make services more fun for worshippers? Would Irish Catholics not mind if you showed your bra straps in church if it meant they could get a few more attendees? Would synagogues in Israel do away with bound copies of the Torah and instead list all of its teachings on iTunes? I was starting to wonder whether a church was still a church if it's bite-sized, sugarcoated, instant, microwavable, disposable. It's clear that for three million people, it isn't this way, or else they don't seem to mind.

"At North Way, there's no dress code. There's no liturgy. There's no strict thing that you have to learn," says Pastor Jay. "There's no in crowd. There's no favoritism of members versus nonmembers. All that makes it very open and inviting to the people who are searching."

That's echoed in Travis's research. "Megachurches are second-chance places," he says. "You find a higher percentage of divorced people, people who have had bankruptcies, people who have been through very tragic situations like the death of a loved one. At a smaller church, the person might feel guilt, embarrassment, shame, judgment, or just not want to go somewhere that everyone knows his history. At a megachurch, you feel acceptance because the church is full of people like this; contemporary megachurches have been clear that they're not looking for perfect people. It's very 'come as you are.' "

Now everyone in the auditorium is standing and clapping and singing more or less in tune. "You are the one I will worship. You are the one I will serve all my days." As far as I understand it, many religions are based on stories of suffering: Jesus's crucifixion, Jews as slaves in Egypt, Siddhartha subsisting on a single grain of rice per day. Megachurches, with their Top 40 soundalike music, their food courts, their comfy chairs and iPod-downloadable sermons, make religion seem easy. Is that why megachurches came along, to meet our desire to have religion become more accessible, more convenient, more entertaining? And is there anything wrong with making religion that way, like nearly everything else in our postmodern lives? If it gets more people into church, some argue, who cares?

"We try to strike a balance between the rich tradition of music in the Christian faith, like the hymns of the eighteenth and nineteenth century, so we do one hymn," says Pastor Jay. "But primarily, we do contemporary Christian music, songs that have been written in the last two decades or so, that capture the sound people might hear if they turned on the radio. It would have a little bit of a beat to it, some rhythm, and the lyrics would make sense—you wouldn't talk about some strange language that they wouldn't understand, like about being 'covered by the blood' or something."

Rick Warren, pastor of California's Saddleback Valley Community Church and author of *The Purpose Driven Life* (which has sold more than 23 million copies), is the king of the megachurch. He runs what some even call a "giga-church," defined as any church with more than 10,000 members. Warren's congregation is actually made up of 20,000 members—so many he rented out the Los Angeles Angels of Anaheim stadium for the church's twenty-fifth anniversary. Otherwise his parishioners couldn't have all met at once (their attendance is usually spread across several weekend services). Over fourteen separate Christmas services, 42,000 worshippers attended Warren's church.

I reached out to Warren to talk about what he thinks his parishioners gain from attending one of the largest churches in the country, and whether there are trade-offs. I heard back from his chief of staff that Warren was "honored by [my] request to interview him for the book," even though he eventually declined. He did bless its "launch and release," though, so that's a plus.

Warren's campus sprawls over 120 acres in Orange County. Journalist Malcolm Gladwell identified one of the most important, conscious tenets of Saddleback: "The church would not look churchy: no pews, or stained glass, or lofty spires. Saddleback looks like a college campus, and the main sanctuary looks like the school gymnasium. Parking is plentiful. The chairs are comfortable. There are loudspeakers and television screens everywhere broadcasting the worship service, and all the doors are open, so anyone can slip in or out, at any time, in the anonymity of the enormous crowds. Saddleback is a church with very low barriers to entry."

Now thanks to its booming membership, leaders from different churches—even different religions—are looking to Warren for help going big. Ron Wolfson, cofounder of Synagogue 3000, an organization that promotes revitalization of Jewish synagogues, is all for borrowing the comfy chairs, dramatic lighting and videos, "greeters" for new worshippers, and five-piece bands of evangelical megachurches. Warren even spoke at the 2007 Union for Reform Judaism's biennial convention; the conference's resounding overall message to leaders of Reform Jewish synagogues was to take a page from the megachurch playbook by adding live music and always welcoming in more newcomers.

* * *

Members I spoke to would probably not use the term "mega-church" to describe North Way, although Pastor Jay did say the word is "more descriptive than pejorative." Still, size is addressed head-on in the Welcome Center pamphlet:

> *Don't let our size scare you; our focus is on church health, not church size. Just as a healthy child will always grow, we believe a healthy, well-balanced church will naturally grow over time. The issue is not really one of church size; there are strong and weak churches of all sizes. There are warm and cold churches of all sizes. Large or small, a healthy, biblical church is one that is focused on Jesus, is biblically rooted, and has people authentically connected into God's family.*
>
> *Also, large churches are quite biblical, with an example being the first church in Jerusalem, which began with 3,000 members, and quickly grew to "tens of thousands," according to the Book of Acts. Most importantly, a large, vibrant church can offer important advantages to your family.*

A few months after I attended services at North Way, I decided I needed to talk to some of its parishioners. I wanted to find out why they chose North Way, what was so great about this church, what it meant to them. I needed to know why they made the decision to be part of such a large institution. For many, a place of worship is not chosen but defaulted to, since it was the church of their parents and grandparents, say, or the church they'd been raised in; people, lots of times including the pastor, would already know their names. But since most megachurches are so new, I can't believe that many people are attending because it's what they were raised on, or that they already had a connection to that church. No, these were brand-new connections, sought out by strangers.

After all, "Most megachurch attendees are first generation," says Travis. "But that's because most megachurches have come about in the past ten or twenty years."

I talked to half a dozen members, who are all very active in the church through weekly services, small-group membership, and extra volunteering like working as a greeter, a "marriage mender," ministering to children, or going on mission trips.

"No matter what you're going through, you're never alone," says Teresa, a middle-aged woman who goes on mission trips through the church.

Raquel, a thirty-five-year-old portfolio manager at an investment firm, also finds strength in numbers. She joined North Way in 2007. "Before that, all of the churches I attended had a hundred members or fewer," she says. "But worship always seems more powerful with more people." Raquel sees other benefits, such as "more small groups to choose from and more ministries—basically, more ways to get involved. You don't have to get involved with something you're not interested in, because there are so many ways to volunteer that you can just choose the ones you *are* interested in." A wide cross-section of people is also appealing socially, especially since Raquel is single. "I'm not limited to a small pool of people to meet, which could lead to a small circle of friends. With all of the different groups, I get to know people I might not ordinarily meet. And I never have to do anything or join anything I don't want to."

That said, Raquel says she did initially have some trouble adjusting to the megachurch. "I admit the first four months were difficult. I would go to services and hang around afterward looking to talk to someone, but I wouldn't have any friends there," Raquel says. She joined a small group, but it wasn't a great fit. "I was starting to wonder if God had really called me to this church," she says. She was getting dangerously close to Pastor Jay's six-month drop-off point. But then she joined a different small group. She started connecting with people she had more in common with and found a few of those friends at services. "That's when I started really feeling like I had people to minister to and who could minister to me," she says. North Way had become her third place.

Back at North Way, emblazoned on the giant screen for the entire hour-and-a-half service, are the words "SHIFT_family." The pamphlet about today's sermon says "SHIFT_marriage." Both are in the same style and font that Nissan uses for its advertising, which flashes "SHIFT_expectations" at the end of every commercial. According to *The Wall Street Journal*, Nissan spent between $700 and $750 million on the SHIFT_campaign. An expert on product branding said it was a great campaign because "it provided a clear, simple, desired mind-set that plainly asks the average person to challenge his perceptions. In short, a very powerful branding exercise that steps into the spiritual." A car commercial can be spiritual?

North Way's SHIFT_family campaign makes for some messy semiotics; why would the church want to silently endorse a specific brand of car? Why would a church adopt a strategy that could make its members, at least subconsciously, associate holiness with Nissanness? It's nothing that sinister, of course, but it's fair to think that North Way may be co-opting a part of pop culture to make its members feel comfortable. It's a way of assigning the church relevance to the larger happenings in the world, especially the world of media. Most people in this audience, myself included, probably watch a lot of TV. It's easier to relate to something we already know, familiar from television, something we all experience just walking around, just overhearing sound bites. You have a church co-opting a message from an advertiser, that is in turn co-opting its message from the realm of spirituality. So I guess it's not just one-sided; faith is drawing from pop culture and pop culture is drawing from faith.

What does it say about us if we want to go to a church that feels like watching TV? What does it say about a church that wants to recruit members by advertising entertainment and convenience? The experience of sitting in these wonderful chairs and staring at a grown woman's baptism on an oversized TV screen isn't far from what most of us would normally be doing on Sundays, complete with commercials. Two videographers sit on spider-legged perches above the audience, turning three dimensions into two as a woman makes a pact with God. Even though it's going on in front of me, I notice that my eyes gravitate toward the two-dimensional experience; rather than watching the real-life people enacting the real-life scene not twenty feet away, I watch it on the giant television.

No matter what you think of megachurches, it looks like they aren't going anywhere. First, their attendees tend to be younger than other church attendees, meaning megachurches don't have to contend with a dying-out population the same way traditional churches do. According to data collected by Travis, roughly every ten years marks a doubling of the ratio of megachurches to Americans. So, for example, in 1990 there were 1.2 megachurches per million of the United States population. By 2000, there was nearly double that—2.19 megachurches per million people; by 2005 there were 4 megachurches per million people. That rate of increase is only predicted to continue.

* * *

Pastor Jay is onstage. Today, his sermon is about marriage. He calls up a couple to talk about their experience: they were on the very verge of divorce, he explains, but their relationships with God and the church helped them through it; they're happy now. As the couple walks up, I watch them on the screens. They have microphones attached behind their ears like Madonna or Janet Jackson in concert.

The choir and musicians have left the stage. The couple makes their way to the pastor. The three of them sit down at a table and chairs set in front of all the music stands. It's a Formica-top table with four chairs arranged around it. A bowl of plastic fruit sits on the table. A kettle and teacups on saucers mark the place settings. A two-foot ceramic Benji sheepdog waits attentively by their feet.

"So, you were sleeping on the couch," Pastor Jay says to the husband. "And that's not a good place to be, is it?"

Pastor Jay then tells a story about a recent dinner he had at Fatburger, and then he segues into a different story about taking his wife to dinner at Outback Steakhouse. It feels like watching television. This is not some buttoned-up priest or rabbi talking, it's just Jay, the guy who eats in the same restaurants as us, drives the same Nissan, wears the same chinos.

Watching the pastor do relationship counseling onstage doesn't feel like snooping on a personal moment, something private between a couple in a rough spot. Watching their images on the screens, in the comfort of my cushioned chair, it feels like watching an episode of *Dr. Phil*, something from the secular world that has little to do with God. It feels like everything I already know from pop culture, something comfortable that could fit into the life I already have. And I can say whatever I want about the impersonal nature of being part of a congregation this large, or about the artifice of sermons on iTunes. In the end, this couple seems genuinely helped by the support they're getting from this pastor, this congregation, this church—megachurch or not.

3.
SALINE AND SILICONE, SUPERSIZED

The plastic surgeon's waiting room is a freak show. Two seats to my left is Miss Tomato, the skin on her face raw and glossy, like the fleshy part of a tomato covered in clear hair gel. From her voice, she sounds grandmotherly—I wonder if she's a chemical peel gone wrong, or a face-lift. After five minutes of filling out forms and trying not to accidentally look to my left, in walks Bubble Head. She has several inches of white gauze wrapped around her head and under her chin, like an old cartoon of someone with a toothache. She wears a green tracksuit, which matches the green, water-balloon things on the sides of her gauzed head— they look like Disney ears. Behind the ears are two small plastic drains, each filled with half an inch of bright red blood; all of this is strapped down under white fishing net fabric. Bubble Head, who could play an alien in a 1950s B movie, is quickly shuffled to a waiting room in the back.

This is not quite the sexy scene I'd imagined. Nearly everyone with whom I've discussed this book (my grandmother being the rare exception) suggested a chapter on penile or breast enlargements; mostly since I felt better acquainted, I decided to write about breasts. I figured that when dealing with such a provocative subject matter, I'd easily find some *Playboy*-ready material. But I forgot about the blood and anesthesia of surgery. I'd pleasantly suppressed the struggle of doing battle with your body and your mind, the issues of body image and self-esteem and societal pressure. For completely unaesthetic reasons, this might end up being the unsexiest supersizing of them all.

I'm in this plastic surgeon's waiting room because more American women get breast enlargements than women anywhere else in the world. The procedure is popular in lots of other countries (especially Brazil, Argentina, Mexico, England, France, and Italy), but America still tops the charts, says Wendy Lewis, author of *Plastic Makes Perfect*. In the past few years, implant popularity has also grown in Asia, especially in China, Japan, Thailand, and South Korea. In survey results from the International Society of Aesthetic Plastic Surgery, breast augmentation was reported to be the most common cosmetic surgery procedure in the world. That American women still get the most enlargements is surprising considering that implants were invented in Asia, not in the United States; also, the FDA's strict rules mean implant innovations come to America only years after they've been widely used in Europe.

According to the *Guinness World Records,* the person who holds the title for most cosmetic surgeries is an American woman named Cindy Jackson, who grew up in Ohio. She's been called a "Living Barbie Doll," having shelled out more than $100,000 on more than fifty cosmetic procedures, including breast enlargements, cheek implants, face-lifts, and a chin reduction. In an interview with ESPN's *Guinness Chat,* she was asked whether she would recommend these kinds of procedures to other people. Jackson talked about plastic surgery like it was the American dream, even an unassailable right: "Don't give up and don't let anyone tell you [that] you can't live up to your dreams," she said.

I'm sitting here in the gray, airline-seat-fabric chair in the plush waiting room of Dr. F, who will soon be feeling me up. Magazines spread on the tables in front of me are either classy, like *Vogue,* or for soccer moms, like *Family Circle.* But rather than read, I'm just sitting here, with Miss Tomato Face and Bubble Head, staring at the fake ficus tree. I picked Dr. F because he's not some quack; on the contrary, he's listed in *The Best Doctors in America* and formerly held an important post at a national surgical association. His Web site says he is "highly regarded by patients and peers for his surgical skill and aesthetic sensibility," and that "his interests include facial surgery, breast surgery, surgery of the abdomen, and liposuction."

I start filling out a stack of paperwork stuck to a clipboard. Check yes or no for a history of glaucoma, stroke, bronchitis, seizures, diabetes, asthma. Fill in the blanks about smoking, drinking, and recreational drug use. Where are the breast questions? The body-image evaluation?

I want to know what it might feel like to go big in the most personal way possible—with your own body. I want to know what it feels like to choose new body parts the same way you'd order a sweater from a catalogue—*I like how it looks on the model, but how will it look on me?* I'm here to try on some double-D-and-up breasts.

Before I see Dr. F, I get called in to see Sherry, the perky, fortyish brunette who coordinates the financing and scheduling of the surgeries. First thing, she tells me she has implants. She expounds on the risks—wrinkling and additional surgery, at the patient's expense, for repairs if "one implant is riding higher than the other." But then she shows me albums of Dr. F's oeuvre, two binders full of photos, each showing a woman naked from the neck to the belly button. They're headless, identityless. They are row after row of huge round, breasts. Some aren't perfect—not exactly symmetrical, or have visible scarring, or sit low on the chest. But one thing is true for nearly all: they're supersized.

"Wow, they're . . . big," I say to Sherry.

"Yeah. You need to go one size bigger than you're comfortable with," she says. Sherry assures me that after three to four months, the implants settle, shrink, and stop feeling so hard.

"I wish I'd gone bigger," she says, looking down at her own chest, covered by a button-down shirt and a blazer. "Most women who come in wish they'd gone bigger. But then they're torn, because they don't want to have to go through the surgery again. They regret not going big enough the first time," she says. Then Sherry wraps her hand around my forearm and looks me in the eyes like she's about to drop a national security secret. "Go big," she whispers. "No one ever says they wish they'd gone smaller."

Sherry also tells me she wishes she'd had the implants inserted from under the breast, rather than through an incision under the nipple. "I fixate on that scar every single time I look in the mirror," she says, sighing. "Every single time."

The office's pamphlets claim a breast augmentation will "improve self-esteem."

In addition to the U.S. producing and getting the most implants per capita, American women also get the largest *size* implants in the world.

"Without a doubt, big implants are an American invention," says Wendy Lewis, the plastic surgery expert. "In America, the average size increase is approximately going from an A to a C. But cup size can be very misleading—that's why doctors think in volume, or cubic centimeters (ccs). The average implant size in the United States is around 350 ccs, while the average size in Brazil and Europe is 200 ccs, and in Asia, much less than that."

So we Americans want 'em big. But in some parts of the country, we want 'em even bigger.

"I see requests for larger implants in Southern California, Texas, Florida, and the rest of the Southeast," says Lewis. "Any beachy lifestyle or warmer climate means body-conscious clothes that show your shape. Cultural preferences of the region also prevail—like, if you live in Orange County or Boca Raton, chances are you know a lot of women with large, perky breasts."

Sherry sends me back to the waiting room. I look around at the empty chairs and think about the risks women are willing to take by sitting in them. A fifteen-year study by the National Cancer Institute found that women with breast implants, versus women who had other cosmetic surgeries, were twice as likely to die from respiratory or brain cancers; these women are also four times likelier to commit suicide. Does breast enhancement make some women want to kill themselves, or do some women who are so unhappy with their appearance as to undergo implant surgery have underlying issues with depression?

Abbie is the cute blond nurse in her mid-twenties. Tanned, thin, and heavily eyelinered, she is a walking billboard for the benefits of plastic surgery. Like a scene from *The Stepford Wives,* all of the women working in the office have pointy, petite faces and shiny hair and round, perfect breasts. I look between the nurses and myself and wonder if everyone can hear the old *Sesame Street* classic line that's blasting in my brain: "One of these things is not like the others!"

I find myself trying to smooth my hair and the wrinkles in my pants on the way back to the exam room.

Now that I've left the waiting-room circus sideshow, I flip through a trashy celebrity tabloid, figuring I'll get some ideas. Celebrities often have to deal with debates about whether their breasts are their own or the work of a surgeon like Dr. F, whose examining room I'm now sitting in, my butt crunching a piece of butcher paper. Lindsay Lohan, Britney Spears, Jessica Simpson, Tara Reid, Mariah Carey, and many other Hollywood starlets insist their breasts are real, despite the dissent of tabloids and Web sites like www.awfulplasticsurgery.com. For celebrities, and even regular gals, the stigma surrounding plastic surgery persists—for some women, not enough to abstain from getting it, but enough to make them deny they got it.

I have on a pink open-front gown. I'm simultaneously bored and nervous, a combination that seems unlikely. I run my hands over the hem of the gown, which is at least soft fabric instead of the stiff papery kind. But I'm used to gowns that open in the back, not split down the front like this one. I try to wrap it across my chest like a bathrobe and hope I'm not accidentally flashing Abbie as she opens the door. Though they may deal mostly in boobs, this is still a doctor's office, not Mardi Gras.

I'm so bored and nervous that I find myself getting wrapped up in my own thoughts. I think about gowns, how it's such a stupid, ill-fitting word to describe what I've got on. A gown sounds beautiful, empowering, elegant, luminous. Ball gowns, evening gowns of taffeta and lace and tulle and sequins, meant to match dinners at the Ritz-Carlton, tuxedos, walks along red carpets. This gown is anything but—I'm embarrassed, exposed, powerless, squirmy. Maybe the point of medical gowns is exactly this, to desexualize, turning erogenous zones like breasts into a canvas of flesh, separate from anything provocative or arousing. Now I'm thinking of bed gowns, fashionable morning attire for eighteenth-century women to wear between their petticoats and aprons. Or wedding gowns, the epitome of female glamour, that special dress for your most special day . . .

I'm so deep in gown etymology that I don't remember Abbie's here until she taps her nails on the counter. Her breasts are round and high, and her hair is blond and straight and perfect. She looks like I imagine Jessica Simpson would if she ever had reason to hold a clipboard. Abbie wastes no time asking what cup size I'd like to go up to.

I blurt out, "Well, I'm really not sure. I kind of want to know about the allure of getting implants, what draws people in and convinces them it's a good idea and the process and all that, and if I would ever get them. If I did get them, I don't know, I'd want nice boobs to fill out my shirts and look good in a bikini top, but I wouldn't want, like, *hel-lo* boobs, like those pole-dancer watermelon things all up under your neck. So a medium-big size, probably, if I really had to narrow it down, but still natural, you know?"

When I'm nervous, I tend to ramble.

Abbie writes on my sheet, *Desired: C*.

I look down at my own chest. I'm pretty comfortable with what I've got, but it makes me wonder: could bigger breasts make me happier, sexier, more secure with my body? It's a thought I instantly banish, don't even let myself think it for more than a second, because as a hyperliterate, postgraduate, empowered woman,

I shouldn't want it, not at all. I know what large fake breasts mean in terms of the hegemonic, patriarchal hierarchy. I also know that most men like big breasts, and that when I go out to the bar, hiding behind my thick-frame glasses and thrift store T-shirt, I make fun of the women with their giant breasts bursting from their tops. "Those are fake, you know that, right?" I say to my male friends who are trying their best not to ogle. In my silent pauses, hidden by the smoke from the bar and reflected in the shine of lipstick, I can admit to myself that I—and perhaps some women like me—want that same attention, for people to look at me the way they're looking at her. It's immediately interrupted by my own internal bark, *You shouldn't want that kind of attention!*

It makes me think of the old adage that negative attention is still better than no attention at all. That's part of why we consume big—a Hummer will draw more attention than a common Corolla, a McMansion more than a town house. Extra-large breast implants are a way to wordlessly, constantly shout, "Look at me!" It's like peacocks unfurling their flashy tails. It's both the spectacle and a means to show your worth, whether reproductive or financial (breast implants typically cost about $7,000). Implants are a much smaller financial investment than a Hummer or a McMansion. But they may be a greater risk to the buyer's health.

Perhaps it's ironic that the first official breast enlargement surgery in America was performed in 1962. That year marked a unique dichotomy between open sexuality and repression, with chaste role models like First Lady Jackie Kennedy leading the public on televised tours of the White House; the death of her nemesis, ultimate busty-girl sex symbol Marilyn Monroe; and the appearance of the first Bond girls in *Dr. No*. Empowered with more options, perhaps women felt free to buy themselves the Barbie boobs they'd always wanted.

The first documented breast enlargement surgeries were performed in Japan, in the 1940s. Hoping to lure American soldiers, Japanese prostitutes injected their own breasts with paraffin, sponges, and nonmedical-grade silicone. Perhaps now, even without consciously knowing the procedure's origins, this is part of the reason we associate large breasts with both sexual willingness and proficiency.

Abbie tells me that breast augmentation is the most popular plastic surgery procedure in America. The complication rate is also one of the highest, though this is something Abbie does not say. One such risk is capsular contracture, where the implants turn hard, rigid, and utterly unbreastlike; I've heard a man describe this as when the breasts feel "like a bag filled with Legos." Abbie explains the 1-percent-a-year chance of the implant leaking, and how that risk increases after ten years. She says these implants will almost definitely need to be replaced within twenty years. The FDA confirms this, warning in its handbook that "breast implants do *not* last a lifetime." In an FDA study from 2000, one-third of women who received implants said that problems caused them to undergo at least one additional surgery to remove or replace an implant.

To feel less intimidated, I remind myself that thousands of women in America make it through this process every year. And it's not just strippers, celebutantes, and wannabe starlets. According to a *Newsweek* article, "The typical implant consumer is not the Hollywood elite or the Las Vegas showgirl but rather is thirty-something, married with a few kids, and has a family income under $70,000."

Abbie tells me about her own experience with breast implant surgery, how during the first day, the pain is simply brutal. Like an elephant sitting on your chest whenever you try to breathe in, she says. She tells me about the gamble anytime you undergo surgery, the risks of anesthesia, bleeding, infection, of having a foreign object in your body. She says how you wake up and see these huge, hard breasts and think they look ridiculous, and how you wish you never got them, and how much you hurt.

"Yeah, it's a roller coaster," Abbie says. "The pain, all the emotion."

I guess my expression is apprehensive.

Then she assures me, "But I would do it all over again in a second. It was totally, completely worth it."

The pain, expense, and health risks don't seem to deter many other patients either, patients who are getting younger and younger. In 1992, only 978 women aged eighteen or younger underwent breast augmentation. By 2004, the number for that same age group nearly quadrupled, jumping to 3,841. The numbers continue to rise. One message comes through to them clearly and unanimously: when it comes to breasts, bigger is better.

"Typically, the younger the woman, the larger the breasts she wants," says Wendy Lewis.

The FDA is concerned about the "growing use of breast implants among teenagers," and cautions against teen breast augmentations. Its clinical trials of unapproved saline and silicone implants actually prohibit them for use on women who are younger than eighteen years old. Worried about the effects of implants that aren't reversible, the FDA warns of the dimpling, puckering, and wrinkling of skin that can result from a teenager having her implants removed. Teens who rush into the decision for the surgery may not be finished developing, or not ready to handle the psychological decision of surgery.

When Dr. F comes into the room, he wants to talk about books, not boobs. He's seen on my chart that I teach college English classes, and he says he's always loved reading and writing, how he loves Willie Morris—have you read Willie Morris?—and Eudora Welty, Faulkner, Capote. His voice is Arkansas-inflected, not hill-billy, but slow and rhythmic, the pace of a rocking chair. He keeps calling me a "lady," and I have to remind myself not to look over my shoulder, half expecting to see Zsa Zsa Gabor. Dr. F is clean-shaven with salt-and-pepper hair and a wide, handsome smile.

After I hear a detailed plot summary for *North Toward Home,* a Willie Morris novel, Dr. F is ready to talk breasts. He opens my gown and takes a long look. He reaches for me and his hands are soft. He squeezes firmly but it doesn't hurt. He presses in a way that reminds me I'm not filled with magic fairy dust, but glands and tissue and blood. It just takes a minute and it's the same exam I've gotten every year at the gynecologist, but it feels different. I'm nervous and I know the sweat is boiling up from my skin, which makes me only more nervous. Dr. F sits back and crosses his arms.

"Do you think your breasts are even, symmetrical?" he asks.

I panic inside. My blood percolates. Are they not? I mean, am I lopsided and I never noticed? The gown sticks to the back of my neck. I'm having trouble swallowing.

Fine, I think. *I've got weird boobs. But I don't need boobs*—I am practically screaming this inside my own head—*I have brains!*

Or is this how they get you—tell you you're messed up, that you need a boob job to fix the damage? First surrounded by Stepfords and then asked one pointed question, my years of enlightened confidence crumble. I'm back to that awkward version of myself from junior high, standing in front of a mirror and leering at my reflection.

I stammer, "Uh, I think so. I guess . . . I've always thought so."

"Me too," he says, and I sigh out loud with relief. "I just wanted to make sure we're looking at the same thing here. Some women seem to have a warped view of how they look."

Yeah, I think, *those poor women with a warped view of how they look,* and I fiddle with a loose string on my gown. He goes on to tell me that my breasts have nice shape and volume, and now I surpass mere breast-acceptance and soar into breast-pride. I see what Abbie means about the roller-coaster effect of self-image, and I haven't even had the surgery.

Dr. F tells me about the practicalities of the one-and-a-half-hour procedure—under-the-muscle implants so you can still breast-feed, implants inserted through a four-centimeter incision under the fold of the breast, saline not silicone, overinflating them so when they settle they're the right size, four to six weeks without exercising, a week without driving, drains for blood in the first twenty-four hours to decrease the chances of wrinkling and hardening.

Then the doctor leaves and Abbie asks if I have any questions. She reminds me she got her implants here.

"Ask me anything," she says. "I mean anything."

"I guess I'm just wondering . . . do they ever look real?"

"If you get the kind that stick out past your armpits, no. Those just look tacky," she says. She cannot believe it when I tell her I've never actually seen bare implant breasts in real life before.

"Don't any of your friends have them?"

"No," I say. She's incredulous.

I want to ask Abbie if after the surgery, you smile when you look in the mirror, or if you just move on to the next thing to obsess over. I want to ask if she finds herself attracted to men who drive Hummers, if she wants to one day live in a giant sprawling suburban mansion. I want to ask if she goes big in other areas of her life, and why she's willing to be a missionary for the "bigger is better" movement.

Instead, I just mumble, "Uh, no."

Then she says, "Okay. I'll show you mine."

She pulls her standard-issue blue scrubs shirt over her head and unhooks her bra before I can blurt out a response. It all happens so fast, and only seconds later, Abbie stands, grinning at me, topless, telling me to examine, to see for myself. Her nipples are stretched and round like pepperoni, but the breasts look natural and perfect; I would never know they were fakes. She lifts one breast in each hand to show me the incision scar underneath, and bounces them a little, saying they feel real. I have the self-conscious realization that I'm in a junior high school boy's fantasy, and, likely sensing my awkwardness from the gaping silence, Abbie puts her bra and shirt back on.

I can easily see how big breast implants can make you lurch toward extremes—low self-esteem, picking yourself apart for not being perfect as a Barbie doll, airbrushed like a Victoria's Secret model. Or instead they make you burst at the seams with confidence, eager to show and tell, basking in your breasts like they're a fabulous new purse or pair of exquisite designer heels. For some women, they're a revelation. As the "Living Barbie Doll" Cindy Jackson first told us, they can help you be who you've always dreamt of being.

Plastic surgeons got excited about a new kind of implant, nicknamed the "gummy bear." Technically, they're known as anatomic high-cohesive silicone-gel implants (which makes clear why a touchy-feely nickname is in order). The implant material is said to be denser and more malleable, better at maintaining its original shape, and less likely to rupture than current breast implants made of silicone or saline. The implant material has been used in Europe for a decade.

They're called gummy bears because they're supposed to be more resilient than saline implants. Like gummy bear candies, when you squeeze them, they're supposed to bounce back to their original shape. Also like the candy, if you cut them, they don't deflate, ooze, or leak.

"Leak" is the most dreaded word in the implant industry. Implants come with bar codes that act as tracking devices in case of defects or recalls. In 1991, a U.S. manufacturer pulled its polyurethane-foam implants from the market; the coating decomposed, releasing a chemical that was potentially carcinogenic. In England, some women with new soybean oil implants started noticing a rancid smell and inflammation—British health authorities found the leaking implant material might be toxic, and suggested by 2000 that all women with this type of implants have them removed. Silicone implants gave Americans a scare in 1992, when the FDA pulled them from the market, saying manufacturers could not "provide adequate evidence that they are marketing a safe product." Silicone implants were said to leak and rupture, causing symptoms similar to those of autoimmune diseases. Currently, silicone implants are available only to women having reconstructive breast surgery, and even then are considered "investigational."

Saline implants, like the ones Abbie has, now dominate the market, but these also are known to leak and deflate like old water beds. They're inserted into the body empty, like little Baggies, and then filled with the saltwater solution after they're inside; gummy bear implants are inserted into the body prefilled with silicone. Criticism of the gummy bear include a harder, less natural feel, and that they may be more difficult for surgeons to implant. But health authorities are excited that at least this kind is less likely to leak.

"Now, the fun part," Abbie says. She hands me a stretchy white sports bra, which seems very unsexy and not fun. But then she hands me my new boobs, smooth plastic filled with silicone, clear and slightly firmer than jelly. They are filled to 250 ccs, what Abbie describes as the "starter size." I squish them in my fist before slipping them into the bra. They make me a cup size bigger, and although it's a change, it's not shocking. I have flashbacks to junior high, stuffing my training bra with tissues, then socks, in hopes of what my teenage years might produce.

While I was growing up, my mom always emphasized confidence, and repeated like a mantra that what God gives you is beautiful. My mom's thin frame also supported D cups, so I figured that might just be something beautiful, well-endowed people said. But I had boyfriends who loved my small boobs, and—except when a Victoria's Secret commercial made me second-guess myself for thirty seconds—so did I. So I figured I'd be, at best, an unlikely candidate for a breast enlargement.

That's why I was surprised when, a week before my appointment with Dr. F, I took a quiz on a breast enlargement information Web site and met exactly half of the markers that make a good candidate for a boob job. The ones I could easily disregard were for weight loss or pregnancy changing my breasts, or for noticeably different-sized breasts. As for "women who are bothered by the feeling that their breasts are too small," for whom "dresses that fit well around the hips are often too large at the bustline," and who "feel self-conscious wearing a swimsuit or form-fitting top," I had to answer yes.

But are there many women out there who don't think their breasts are too small, or who don't feel self-conscious in a swimsuit? Didn't most of us stand in front of a mirror in junior high school—or, more recently, under the fluorescent lights of a dressing room—and wish our bodies looked different? Does that really make nearly all women good candidates to go under the knife for bigger breasts?

Abbie suggests I try a size bigger, reiterating Sherry's words to go one step up from where I feel comfortable, in order to account for settling and shrinking. She hands me a 350 ccs pair and suggests for my surgery, the doctor inflate them to 380 ccs. I nod, trying to focus on what she's saying despite two foreign objects in my bra that feel like raw chicken cutlets.

When I look down, I laugh. I can't see my stomach—just round, perfect, ballooning boobs. I look like Pamela Anderson. I look like Jenna Jameson. I'm a funhouse mirror version of myself, and

I start to freak out and want to take off the silicone Frisbees, to throw the empty bra on the floor, to tell Abbie I'm just doing field research, and that what I personally most want in this instant is to flee past Miss Tomato Face and Bubble Head and run out of the office and drive away and never think about any of this again.

And as all this races through my head and I'm sweating on the silicone, I catch another glance of myself in the mirror on the wall; I still can't believe it's me. I stare intently, flipping between my chest and my face. I look like a different person. Only now, it's more Marilyn Monroe and less Jenna Jameson than I'd thought. The shock fades to romance. I can imagine how many women have stood in this room, or rooms like this all across America, feeling the same way. I put on my tank top, the one that I don't even have to wear a bra with and that makes my breasts look flat and unassuming. Over the 350 ccs bra, my chest (or a chest that I could have for $5,700 and a week off work) is now transformed: resplendent, glorious, holy. I can't stop looking at myself—forward, in profile, profile from the other side.

And suddenly, I'm sold.

Big is good. Big is goooood.

Abbie watches me, as excited and hypnotized as I am.

"Those are great on you," she chirps.

"Yes," I say. "Yes, they are."

With such a large chest, my stomach is less noticeable and my hips look slimmer. Implants this large would make me a more physically ideal woman, an embodiment of what's considered attractive. I'm convinced I wouldn't have many bad days if I looked like this. I guess you could say I would probably be in the category of women thrilled with themselves via their new breasts. I am thrilled with these chicken cutlets, and they're only floor samples.

"Yeah, those are definitely it," says Abbie. "Look at you!"

And that's exactly the problem. I can't stop looking.

It's getting awkward, me staring at myself.

Abbie starts tapping her nails on the counter.

"So, you're all ready then?" she asks. It's clear that she's getting ready to finish my paperwork, to go to the next exam room where she will also admire and coo, fanning away another woman's doubts like bothersome gnats.

I reach inside my shirt and hand Abbie each silicone breast, squishy and still warm from my body. The bra she gave me now hangs on my frame, deflated and wrinkly. I feel like I'm missing something, but it doesn't feel like a lost wallet, or the expectation of waiting to get a letter from an old friend. Instead, it's a kind of deep, panicked absence—I don't just want them back, I *need* them. It makes me wonder how many women who come for a consultation actually return for the surgery. Though Dr. F's office wouldn't tell me exactly what percent, they do say "most." And I can see why all the cautions and the numbers, the price tag and the health risks, are so much easier to scoff at when I sit in my office, reading them on my computer. Here, they are easy to dismiss—a handsome, charming, reassuring doctor; a photo album of perfect, real-life Barbie boobs; the possibility of replacing a disappointing small or medium "before" with the perfect extra-large "after."

I feel none of the same elation about my own, natural body as I had about the artificial one. This is an ugliness I haven't felt since my preteen years, something I was sure I'd grown out of— forgotten along with my locker combination and the capital of

North Dakota. I thought this experiment would confirm how the cost and the risks women undertake to supersize their breasts are silly, useless. But standing here in this empty bra, I understand how easy it is to be lured into this form of supersizing, and how difficult it is to expunge insecurities, the kind that even decades later continue to leak.

4.
WHAT HAPPENS IN VEGAS

'm lost. Two (carpeted) roads diverged in a neon casino, and I, I took the one that led to the Grand Pool complex. Wherever it is I've ended up features rows of slot machines that whirr, ring, and flash sevens and cherries. People laugh and scream at the booth selling six-dollar shots of Jägermeister, or ones mixed with Red Bull for an extra two bucks. It's amusement-park loud and neon bright, no clock, window, or door in sight. I'm starting to feel as if I will never find the hallway I need, which would take me to the elevator I need, which would take me up to another hallway, where I could eventually find my room and put this long first day in Las Vegas to rest.

I've had only two margaritas, so they're probably not to blame for why I can't find my room. My guess is that it's because this hotel, the MGM Grand, is the largest hotel in America. It has 5,690 rooms, and for 5,689 of them my electronic room key won't work. All in all, the hotel has about 18,000 doors.

Walking around the property, I pass the pool complex, which covers nearly seven acres. I make a mental note to rent a tube the next day to ride the quarter-mile-long "lazy river" that snakes around one of the half-dozen pools. I pass the Grand Spa, which sprawls over 28,000 square feet. I walk past the entrance to the Monorail, built to connect the various hotels and attractions, with a stop to access every destination on the Strip; the MGM

Grand is the only hotel with two different stops. The following night, I'll have drinks and go dancing at Studio 54, the hotel's 20,000-square-foot nightclub, which is not to be confused with its two lounges. Then there are the three theaters that host a burlesque show, a Cirque du Soleil show, and a rotating celebrity show. I pass the hall with the classic Vegas all-you-can-eat buffet. I see a sign for the valet-taxi stand, which is actually wider, and has more lanes, than California's Orange County Freeway. The hotel has so many rooms that if you wanted to spend one night in each, it would take you thirteen years and eight months. If all of the 7,778 beds were stacked up, the pile would stand more than two miles high, more than ten times as tall as the Empire State Building. I stop to take out my cell phone, wishing I had one with GPS that could map me back to my room. The phone's wallpaper is a new photo I took on the way into the hotel of me with the hotel's iconic, 45-foot-tall, 100,000-pound lion statue, the largest bronze statue in America. After getting this lost, though, I am a little less impressed by size.

Ten mindless minutes of wandering later, I get sidetracked by an area called Studio City. It's not so much the CBS and MTV merchandise that pulls me in, as it is a room where they host screenings of TV pilots—a cool, dark room in which someone who's sweaty and jet-lagged and had two margaritas could easily take a nap. I try to make a pit stop, but the greeter ultimately says he can't let me in because I checked on the demographic form that I work in the media, and "the networks don't want people writing about these pilots before they get tested." Fine—no nap for the weary. Then I pass a hair salon. I see a sign for the arena, which seats 15,000 people. I keep walking, looking for markers that might point me toward my temporary home, until I nearly smack into a throng of people, all crowded around and craning to see something. Turns out, they're looking at lions. Real live lions. It's the Plexiglas Lion Habitat—in the middle of the hotel. It makes me want to find a dog just so I could say to it, "Toto, we're not in a normal hotel anymore."

The MGM Grand is not just some supersized outlier in an otherwise average-sized town. Of the twenty largest hotels in the world, fifteen of them are in Las Vegas, all packed into a two-mile radius. Perhaps it's not surprising, since Vegas has made its reputation as the home of the extreme—alcohol served and consumed twenty-four hours a day, surgically enhanced DDD Barbie boobs on (legal) prostitutes, desert temperatures, 240-foot-high blasts from the Bellagio's fountains. The 2009 *Washington Post* article "In Vegas, It's Easy to Live XXL" described the city as "an around-the-clock Mecca to excess . . . [it] invites and defines excess. There are excessive displays of conspicuous consumption everywhere."

After all, this town is home to the world's largest martini (twenty gallons of gin) and the world's largest bikini parade (three hundred preapproved gals clomping down the Strip). It has the Sapphire, billed as the world's largest gentleman's club, which runs the Sapphire Pool at the Rio, the world's largest topless pool. Vegas hosts the World Series of Poker, not surprisingly the world's largest poker tournament. The city has the world's largest gift shop, the Bonanza Gift & Souvenir Shop, on the corner of Sahara Avenue and Las Vegas Boulevard, which sells shot glasses and instructional books on pole dancing. The city boasts the world's largest chocolate fountain, twenty-seven feet tall and constantly swirling 2,100 pounds of chocolate, at the Bellagio's Jean Philippe Patisserie. In other big food, Vegas is home to the world's largest burrito, two feet long and weighing six pounds, served at the NASCAR Café at the Sahara. It costs $19.99, but if you can finish one, it's free. Las Vegas also has some of the country's highest marriage, divorce, and suicide rates. Viewed from space, it is the brightest metropolitan area on earth. And since the city is ranked as one of the fastest-growing regions in America, Vegas looks like it's only going to get bigger.

The next morning, trying to get some coffee and a bagel—at any one of the hotel's three Starbucks—I'm lost again. I don't even have margaritas as an excuse anymore, and now I've been checked into the hotel for twenty-four hours, so my complete disorientation seems to be bordering on ridiculous. I pass the Rainforest Cafe, with an animatronic alligator launching itself at me from a plastic pond. I walk by a boutique gift shop and then the West Wing bar, a swanky (and at 9:00 A.M., completely empty) lounge of leather couches and throw pillows and moody red lighting. As someone who was not blessed with an exceptional sense of direction, I've certainly been lost before, but I usually manage fine. In fact, as far as I can remember, I've never been lost in a hotel before, at least not more than a moment or two of disorientation. But this morning, I'm stone-cold sober and am so lost that I contemplate lying down on the floor and waiting for a kind employee to come pick me up and escort me to my coffee.

Finally, I spot it—one of the overhead signs promising Starbucks. Several wrong turns later (since the overhead signs only mention destinations sporadically) I arrive. Hallelujah! Once I've got my breakfast in hand, I try to retrace my steps to get back to my room. I remember passing a bar, but was it the Rouge Bar or the

Centrifuge Bar? I walk down a few long hallways, and I'm in the middle of the casino, tables and slots surrounding me in every direction. The casino has more than 145 table games and 3,000 slot machines, all with competing noises and flashing lights, spread out across more than 170,000 square feet, about the size of four football fields. I'm officially lost in Casinoville. There are more than 800 decks of cards being shuffled here at any given moment, and they go through 1,475 decks a day. Games start at $5 a hand and go up to $150,000 per hand for baccarat, plus a few games with even weirder names, like blackjack shoe and pai gow.

The MGM Grand is so big—and as a result, can offer so much to do—that the hotel itself can become a destination.

"It's a very large campus. It's almost a city within itself," says Tim Kelly, vice president of hotel operations, when we sit down in his office. Tim is a handsome guy with thick, slicked-back hair and a legal pad with handwritten bullet points, though he never seems to refer to it. "Even though it's tempting to at least venture out to the Strip, I'm sure there are customers who barely leave the hotel property or stay here the entire time. It's not like when people don't leave their resorts because, say, they're in a remote location. We have everything you need for the course of your stay under one roof. You could relax at the pool, get a massage at the spa, get your hair done at the salon, catch a show, and have a great dinner—you can very easily do all that and still be encapsulated within the property."

Cheryl is a forty-something woman from the Los Angeles area who comes to Vegas twice a year with her husband, Bill, who is currently smoking a cigar in the lobby. She says they always stay at the MGM Grand and usually "drive right up to the hotel, park, and do stuff here until we leave. We go to the pool all day, then at night we go out to dinner here. Afterwards we go to a show or the casino, have a few drinks, and do the same thing the next day but with a different restaurant or different games. We've already seen the Strip, and when you've only got a few days, it's easier just to relax in one place."

I tell her about how I'm always lost here, and ask if that gets better with multiple visits. "You're a smart girl," she says, patting her hand on my shoulder. "Nothing in Vegas is designed for rocket scientists. You'll figure it out." Then she and Bill walk off, headed for the pool.

Of course, Tim tells me the hotel staff's "never-say-no" service, basically akin to "the customer is always right, or can at least order a daiquiri from the pool," is its most important selling point for customers. But he also believes the sheer size of the hotel is a real benefit to its guests. "This way, we can be everything to everyone," he says, unknowingly echoing Pastor Jay of North Way Church. "There's always something different for you to do. It's not like, 'Well, we ate in the restaurant here, so now we have to go somewhere else,' which is sometimes what you're forced to do in the normal hotel world. Here you can spend a week and still not have ventured into all our restaurants."

He's definitely right about that. During my five-day stay—which many people told me was too long, causing me to likely "OD on Vegas"—I went to a different one of the hotel's eateries for drinks and lunch and dinner, and still hit fewer than half of its twenty-something restaurants, not to mention its thirty-something bars. Aside from just being home to the world's largest martini and burrito, eating and drinking is big business in Vegas, and that's definitely true at the MGM Grand, which serves 30,000 meals every day. That amounts to more than 18 million eggs, 208 tons of coffee, and nearly 4.4 million donuts each year, and that's just for breakfast. Dishwashers clean 16 million dishes a year. Every day, the hotel goes through 700 pounds of bacon; 600 pounds of ham; 1,600 pounds of crab legs; 400 pounds of mushroom salad; and 74 gallons of ranch dressing. The MGM Grand Bakery is one of the largest in Las Vegas, operating twenty-four hours a day to prepare baked goods for the hotel. Every day, the bakery pumps out 3,000 croissants, thousands of cookies, and 300 pies, going through 70 gallons of cream. You could feel stuffed just thinking about it. And it's no surprise that drinking is big in Sin City, with the hotel serving 128,000 bottles of vodka a year—plus four million bottles of beer, which breaks down to more than 11,000 bottles a day.

The first real hotel on the Strip—though it wasn't the Strip then— was the Flamingo, which opened in 1946. The first modern "mega-resort casino," the Mirage, didn't open until 1989. When the MGM Grand was built in 1993, its biggest draw, and one that was heavily marketed, was that it was the world's largest hotel.

But actually, "When you're in the hospitality business, you don't want to be known as the largest," Tim says. "You want to be known as the best in service. That's part of why we transitioned away from it." He's referring to the hotel's move in the late '90s to stop marketing itself as the largest hotel and instead focus on what Tim calls the "energy, entertainment, and excitement of the brand."

Perhaps it wasn't so difficult to distance itself from size because "the property stands out more for its color," a rich glowing green at night, "than it does for its size and scope," says Tim. "It doesn't *look* the largest, like some towering property. But when the MGM

Grand was initially built, it looked very big. At the time, the other property that looked very large was the Excalibur. But now that you've seen other buildings go vertical over the past decade, it's really distorted your sense of size when looking at the skyline. Now there are sixty-story towers, and we're only thirty stories. But we're very wide, very expansive. The Venetian, Palazzo, Wynn Encore, Bellagio, and the Mandalay Bay are broken up into separate towers—we're the only one with everything under one roof."

Megahotels, and really everything else in Vegas, continued to do big business until the recession hit, walloping tourism across the country. In 2009, visitor numbers for Las Vegas were down nearly 10 percent from a year before. The major casinos also earned 17 percent less from gamblers in the first three months of 2009, compared to the same period in 2008, according to Nevada regulators. Everyone who heard I was going to Vegas made some comment about what a deal I must've gotten (I didn't), saying that both room rates and airfare prices were down to entice Vegas visitors. It wasn't that I expected a Western ghost town, the Strip empty except for a few stray tumbleweeds. But I didn't brace myself for a crush of people—wasn't this the grand expanse of the West?—that matched exactly what I'd left behind in New York City. Yet the MGM Grand seemed full to the point of being crowded. Getting to the pool or a restaurant meant wading through huge crowds of people.

"At your average hotel, if you ran 60 or 65 percent occupancy on an annual basis, that would be considered a successful, active property. In Vegas, ideally you want to run in the nineties." As in, 90 percent of all of the MGM's rooms would be booked? Even deep in the recession in July 2009, the Wynn and Encore both reported 90 percent occupancy. That seems staggering to me—I hadn't really believed that a hotel this big would be something other than a spectacle, that it could actually be practical.

"The MGM Grand actually runs at about 96 percent occupancy," Tim says, "even in this economy. And there are plenty of days where we run full, even without a big draw like an event or holiday."

A capacity of 96 percent of its more than 5,000 rooms seems like a lot of people, and that's just at one of a dozen of these mega-hotels within a two-mile stretch. Tim estimates that on an average day, there are between 10,000 to 15,000 guests staying at the hotel, plus another 60,000 visitors coming onto the Grand's property to see a boxing match at the arena, catch a show, attend an event at the convention center, eat at one of the restaurants, check out the lions, gamble at the casino, or even hang out at Wet Republic, the $20-a-day nightclublike pool.

A large part of why Vegas hotels can maintain such a high occupancy rate is due to convention traffic. "We were once just a little small gambling town in the desert," says Tim. "But in the late '90s, we started to see another opportunity available to us with conventions and business travelers. That's when it really became a focal point for this city. We realized that during the week, you could generate a lot of money by having great meetings and functions and events, and somewhere like the MGM Grand can house three thousand of your attendees all under one roof, rather than splitting people up in different sites. And space is inexpensive here when you compare Las Vegas to somewhere like San Francisco, New York, or Chicago."

During the week, conventions mean that each room usually houses just one person. Friday through Sunday, though, you get "weekend warriors," says Tim, and rooms are more densely occupied with couples, families, or groups. "Las Vegas is constantly making itself over to attract more and different people. Everyone's added world-class restaurants, entertainment, and shopping," he says. "It's come a long way from being a one-stop gambling town in the desert."

After three days in Vegas, and most of it spent within the campus of the MGM Grand, my mission is to spend the day at the pool, doing no reporting at all; I decide I will not initiate conversations with anyone besides the bikini-clad waitresses who can bring me frozen daiquiris. To live out today's dream, though, I need to find my way from my hotel room on the twelfth floor—using one of the hotel's ninety-three elevators—to the pool complex. I get down to the main floor, where I'm plunked back into the middle of the whirring, blipping, flashing casino, and I feel at least 80 percent sure I should turn right. I do, and I keep walking. I pass Diego, the Mexican restaurant where I had dinner last night. I walk past the food court with the McDonald's and the Nathan's, and one of the Starbucks. I don't want to applaud myself too loudly, but I think that after three days, I might finally be mastering the layout of this expansive 120-acre obstacle course—or at the very least finally able to get myself to the pool without having to stop to ask for directions.

The day before, when I'd mentioned to Tim that I was having a hard time finding my way around, he said, "Maybe initially you can be overwhelmed to a slight degree on the size, thinking *Geez, it looks big*, but it's laid out very well. Once you start to find your way around, it's pretty easy." Easy for someone with a better sense of direction than me, clearly, or someone who carries a compass. Tim also noted that the MGM Grand has one of the highest customer-return rates. I thought better of telling him that sure, it's partially the amenities and the service, but more than anything, people probably don't want to have to figure out how to get around a new hotel.

I walk through the end of the casino and past Studio City, the TV screening place. I pass a few more restaurants that look familiar, and I hope I'm going the right way. That's when I see it—the blinding glow of natural sunlight coming through the giant glass doors that lead out to the pool area. Huzzah! Just in time for me to head home, I think I've finally figured this place out. I decide to celebrate with an $8 inner tube ride down the lazy river.

In 2000, the MGM Grand lost its title as the largest hotel in the world when the First World Hotel opened in Malaysia, boasting 6,118 rooms, a casino, arcade, waterpark, and even an indoor free-fall simulator. I wanted to know if being knocked to number two affected the Grand.

"It wasn't that big an issue for us," says Tim. "A lot of people don't know the First World exists. If you took a poll, most people would still think we're the largest hotel in the world. I mean, we recognize that the First World is there, but we're not planning to expand to retake the title or anything. We're proud of our size, but it's not a competition. Plus, we're still the largest hotel in North America."

There are some big developments in Vegas that have struggled to the point of halting construction. A 2009 *New York Times* article noted: "On the Strip, near Circus Circus, is the yawning emptiness of the $4.8 billion, 87-acre Echelon project, halted last August along with its twelve to fifteen new restaurants. The unfinished,

mirrored eyesore of the $2.9 billion 3,815-room Fontainebleau
tower across from Circus Circus, looms over the city like a prophecy. It went bankrupt and took 6,000 jobs with it." Still, don't
think Vegas construction is paused; in December 2010, the MGM
Mirage-Dubai World project opens "the $8.5 billion CityCenter.
Bristling with construction cranes and gleaming in the 100-degree
sun, the CityCenter casino, hotel, convention center, mall, residential and entertainment metropolis looks like a hallucinogenic
sixty-seven-acre Red Grooms parody of the Las Vegas Strip. The
development spans a quarter-mile, from the Bellagio to the Monte
Carlo Resort and Casino."

Robert Goldstein, the president of the Venetian, told *The New
York Times* he keeps a framed cover of a *Life* magazine from June
20, 1955, that showed casino cancan dancers and warned: "Las Vegas—Is Boom Overextended?" Obviously we've been worried
about Vegas before, and obviously Vegas has risen from our worries, even bigger and more glittery than before. "Las Vegas is down
a bit now, and right now the town is overbuilt," Goldstein says.
"But do you really think all of this is going to fade away and go to
black?"

5.
ENGAGEMENT RING BLING

'm at the Tiffany & Co. flagship store on the corner of Fifth Avenue and Fifty-seventh Street in Manhattan. Its gray stone facade is epic, as much a part of a modern girl's idea of New York landmarks as the Empire State Building or the Statue of Liberty. This Tiffany's is so iconic largely because it has been featured in chick flicks with beloved actresses, from *Sweet Home Alabama* (where Patrick Dempsey—McDreamy himself—closes down the store so Reese Witherspoon can privately pick out any ring she wants), to *Sex and the City* (where the perfect Charlotte York can pick out any ring she wants), to the classic *Breakfast at Tiffany's*, in which Audrey Hepburn as Holly Golightly eats a pastry while admiring the store's window displays. The centerpiece of happiness in the 2009 movie *Bride Wars* is one hunk of a Tiffany Novo ring.

On the other side of the gold revolving door, the first floor of Tiffany's swarms like a hive. This is where they keep showpieces with the ooh-aah factor, like five-carat diamond engagement rings, down to the under $1,000 silver items like charms and keychains. I maneuver through the three-deep rows of gawking tourists and teenage girls trying to convince their mothers to buy them Elle Woods's signature heart necklace from *Legally Blonde*. Since I have an appointment with Mr. R, I take the elevator up to the second floor. When the doors slide open, it's a vastly different scene from what's going on only twenty feet below. Here are the real customers, just a few couples gazing down into well-lit displays, speaking so quietly it feels more like a museum than a retail store.

In addition to crisscrossing the country doing research for this book, I've also been doing a lot of traveling recently for friends' weddings. In fact, I've attended half a dozen of them this year alone. I've been a maid of honor once and a bridesmaid twice. The way each of these scenes started is with my female friend showing me the ring, either in person or a photo on e-mail or Facebook; either way, the ring itself seems as important a part of the equation as the commitment it represents. I also noticed the sheer size of the engagement rings growing, evidenced by how much larger my friends' rings are than their mothers' or grandmothers'.

That's due, at least in part, to the fact that couples are getting married later. One theory is that they're likely more established in their careers by then and better able to drop serious money on a ring. But most of my friends getting married are twenty-six to thirty-one, still renting apartments and trying to make payments on their student loans. I wanted to know why, especially as marriages have gotten shorter, the rocks on engagement rings have gotten bigger.

For several decades, a round-cut diamond engagement ring has reigned as the most popular style. But the average *size* of the diamond has ballooned. Thirty years ago, most engagement rings were half a carat, and one carat was considered large; these days, jewelers are seeing more and more requests for two- and three-carat diamonds. But the one-carat ring has become the new standard, with sales of that size jumping 80 percent from 1996 to 2006. Jewelers have also noticed a bump in brides-to-be wanting the main diamond of the ring encircled in smaller diamonds—a "halo effect" intended to make the main stone look even bigger. The average engagement ring now costs $4,435. A 2006 article in *Modern Jeweler* pointed out that they were seeing "a lot more engagement ring upgrades, where people move to bigger diamonds as affluence increases." The Diamond Information Center estimates that in 2006 alone, 84 percent of brides (that's 2.2 million women) received a one carat or larger ring. The organization also expects diamond engagement rings to grow at roughly 4 percent a year until 2016, when the baby boomers' kids average thirty-one years old.

When the cost of a typical American wedding hovers at $28,000, is it any surprise that the engagement ring is just as big a production?

A Tiffany's greeter walks up to me before I've made it ten feet into the engagement and wedding ring floor. He helps me find Mr. R, a barrel-chested, middle-aged sales associate with a hearty laugh and meticulously groomed eyebrows. Mr. R shakes my hand and asks me what kinds of rings I'm interested in trying on, and I tell him I have no idea. With him on the inside of the square cases filled with glittering diamonds and me following him along the outside of the cases, we cruise past the extra-rare yellow and pink diamonds as big as a quarter and past the miniscule "under $10,000" section.

"Then let's start with the classic Tiffany's setting," he says, sliding open the waist-level case. "It's our biggest seller."

He produces a ring, placing it on a black velvet tray, which I then pick up and slide down my left ring finger. The platinum setting shines, polished to perfection; the prongs rise with outstretched arms around a glimmering 1.6-carat square-cut diamond.

As a former nail biter, I turn my palm facing me and curl in my fingers when I want to look at them. But with a diamond ring on, I find myself stretching my arm out the whole way and looking at the back of my hand, a comically feminine pose of self-worship.

Though it's beautiful and impressive, it's still not nearly as massive as some of the rocks I've seen on engagement rings of friends and coworkers. Ashley, for example, has a platinum band adorned with a round-cut three-carat diamond. When her then-boyfriend, a thirty-year-old attorney, proposed to Ashley, she was "definitely surprised at the size of the diamond." But, she says, "I wouldn't change a thing about it because, bottom line, it's from my husband. He spent months researching and working with a jeweler to get a ring with excellent clarity and color. We say it has 'sizzle.'"

Ashley says that the showstopping size of her ring isn't a big deal to her—though she will admit that it has sometimes been a distraction to others, even to the point of them embarrassing her about it. She remembers the first day she went into work wearing the ring. "I had a big meeting that day, and I was nervous because I was by far the most junior person there—and on top of that I had to do a presentation. When my colleagues noticed the ring, there were the usual questions and answers about it, how he proposed, that kind of thing. Then the meeting started, and in the middle of my presentation, a colleague—male and twice my age—blurted out, 'Jesus, Ashley, how big is that thing?' It was meant to be a harmless tease, but I got so red and flustered, I botched the second half of my PowerPoint."

For Ashley's bachelorette party, friends took her to a drag queen show, where she was pulled onstage for some audience participation. "When he grabbed my hand to take me onstage, he must have felt my ring, because he said, 'What the F is this?' Then in front of everyone, he asked if my fiancé was Jewish, a drug dealer, or a mafia boss. When I said no, he yelled, 'This bitch has got a big-ass ring on—don't anyone rob her!' It was possibly the most miserable experience of my life. Even though I had a sense of humor about it, I'm shy—getting called out like that was just too much for me."

It seems that by wearing a supersized diamond, lots of other people—especially strangers and acquaintances—think they have a right to comment on it. Ashley mentions a conversation she and her husband had with a passing stranger that started out casual—until the woman saw Ashley's ring. "The woman says, 'Finally, a ring I can talk about! I feel bad that so many girls these days are getting little trinket rings.'" Then the woman "proceeded to bombard us with questions about cut, color, carats—even slapping her hands against my ears and prodding my husband for the price. But she never once asked about our story, how we met, or our wedding. It was all about the ring."

In general, diamonds, especially those from Tiffany's, used to be exclusively for the ultrarich, adorning only celebrities like Marilyn Monroe or members of America's wealthiest families; Tiffany's was known for outfitting such legends as the Astors, the Vanderbilts, the Posts, the Huttons, and the Morgans. Today's equivalent, perhaps the Trumps or the Hiltons, are of course still drenched in diamonds, as evidenced by Paris Hilton's twenty-four-carat engagement ring from shipping heir Paris Latsis, circa 2005; Ben Affleck's six-carat pink diamond for JLo; or Heidi Klum's twelve-carat yellow diamond rock from Seal.

But thanks to credit cards, loan availability, and perhaps a rise in female expectations, diamonds have become ever more common. In 1938, diamond seller De Beers first suggested that a man spend two months' salary on an engagement ring. Today's guidelines declare that he spend three months' salary—or more. A fifth-generation jeweler told *Modern Jeweler* that among today's ring buyers, "the price acceptance is mind-boggling. Fifteen or twenty years ago, you hit the ceiling at $1,000, maybe $1,500. We get kids in college and they're not even batting an eyelash at three times that figure." In terms of demand, research shows women have become more and more vocal over the years about which ring they want. A recent study showed that 80 percent of engagement ring buyers were couples, rather than the man picking it out himself. While diamonds have always been the providence of the wealthy, people are spending more on engagement rings than ever before.

Diamond engagement rings have certainly gotten more democratic since their inception in the ninth century, when Pope Nicolas I made a sort of practical betrothal requirement of a man giving his bride-to-be a gold ring to demonstrate the groom's ability to provide for her financially. In 1215, Pope Innocent III declared the need for a longer waiting period between betrothal and marriage, which meant even more couples got engagement rings. Pope Innocent III also widened the engagement ring requirement to allow for silver and iron. Wealthy aristocratic men, needing to show how much more they could afford than common men could, began giving their fiancées gold or silver bands with gems, which served as important status symbols. The gems were so important, in fact, that laws were passed to keep anyone besides the privileged from wearing such ornate jeweled rings.

The first recorded diamond engagement ring was given in 1477 by Archduke Maximilian of Austria to Mary of Burgundy. Diamonds became far more widespread—still solely among the super-rich, of course—in the late nineteenth century, when huge diamond deposits were discovered in Africa.

These days, a diamond engagement ring is standard, even a given; the size of the diamond is the real variable. In part, more available credit in terms of loans and credit cards means couples have access to more expensive rings. And rings are getting larger as just one arm of the whole wedding industry, which is growing exponentially. It's estimated that $40 to $70 million is spent annually on weddings. The average honeymoon costs $3,800. Borders and Barnes & Noble stock countless bridal magazines. Couples invite, on average, 175 wedding guests. Somewhere between a third and half of all couples hire a wedding planner.

There's a special pressure placed on the engagement ring, since it sets the tone for the lavishness—or lack thereof—for the wedding. For example, a 2004 study done by an investment company in the United Kingdom found that 70 percent of women did not want their partners to propose until they had saved enough money to buy the ring of their dreams, and even 28 percent of women they surveyed said they would turn down a proposal if the ring wasn't to their taste.

While I'm standing with my arm outstretched, admiring how good my hand looks with a rock on it, Mr. R suggests that we go bigger. We consider the same style but with a two-carat stone. I don't know if it's just because it's bigger—as Mr. R says it's about equal in terms of colorlessness—but it sparkles so brilliantly, it almost demands a cartoon *ting!* sound. The size of the diamond makes my fingers suddenly look long and slim and graceful, like those of a hand model.

Still, I decide to switch to something even sparklier one case down. It's the Tiffany Novo, which Mr. R says is their second biggest seller, and the lusted-after ring from *Bride Wars*.

Unlike the simple, clean lines of the classic setting, the Novo is flashier: now the square-cut single diamond sits on a thin band of pavé diamonds, where tiny diamonds are placed so close together you can't see the band. Still, it's not as flashy as the Legacy setting, where the center diamond has pavé diamonds *surrounding* it in a square as well as on the band). Mr. R hands me a Novo with a center stone of just more than two carats. I slide it on my finger and it's perfect.

"But is it over-the-top?" I ask, knowing I want him to tell me it's as perfect as I think it is. "Is it too big?"

"No," Mr. R assures me. "Go over two and a half carats and it gets very formal, like a cocktail ring. But you want to be able to wear it all the time, so between two and two and a half is perfect."

"It's beautiful, but that's still pretty big."

"It's not that big," he says. "One carat used to be the standard, but now two carats is standard. Most of our buyers don't go smaller than one and a half carats anymore—they go between one and a half and two and a half carats."

Of course, engagement rings in America didn't start out with two-and-a-half-carat diamonds. The Puritans didn't believe in wearing any kind of jewelry (too showy). In fact, these early Americans' engagement rings were remnants of thimbles. A man would give his fiancée a thimble so that she could use it as she sewed to make her dowry. To show that she'd paid her dowry, come wedding time, the tip of the thimble was cut off and the bottom of the thimble would be worn as a wedding ring.

When times were lean in America, such as during the Great Depression, people cut back on expensive, ostentatious jewelry. That's when filigree engagement rings—all intricate metalwork and no diamond or stone—became popular. During World War II, platinum settings went out of production; the material was banned for civilians so it could be used for the military.

"Prior to the twentieth century, engagement rings were strictly luxury items, and they rarely contained diamonds," said a *Wall Street Journal* article by Rebecca Zerzan called "Five Beloved Traditions Invented to Make You Buy Stuff." Diamond engagement rings came into vogue for regular folks in 1939, when De Beers enlisted the help of ad agency N. W. Ayer & Son. "The [diamond] industry had taken a nosedive in the 1870s, after massive diamond deposits were discovered in South Africa. But the ad agency came to the rescue by introducing the diamond engagement ring and quietly spreading the trend through fashion magazines," Zerzan writes. But diamond engagement rings "didn't become de rigueur for marriage proposals until 1948, when the company launched the crafty 'A Diamond Is Forever' campaign. By sentimentalizing the gems, De Beers ensured that people wouldn't resell them, allowing the company to retain control of the market. In 1999, De Beers chairman Nicky Oppenheimer confessed, 'Diamonds are intrinsically worthless, except for the deep psychological need they fill.'"

These days, even bargain chains like Target, Walmart, Sam's

Club, and Costco are all looking to fill that deep psychological need with blingy engagement rings and wedding supplies. The average price for a ring from Sam's Club is a costly $3,000, though the store's senior diamond buyer told MSNBC those were mostly sold to couples on their second or third marriages; first-timers usually insist on bigger.

My friend Paula is one of those first-timers ("only-timers!") with a big ring: two point eight carats. It has pavé diamonds glittering around the main stone, which is a cushion cut, between a square and a rectangle; it's a rarer shape than the superpopular square or round cuts. Most cushion-cut stones are large; it's difficult to find those diamonds in smaller sizes, especially at one carat or less. Paula says her ideal ring came from *Sex and the City:* "The Harry Winston ring Carrie got from Aidan was beyond exquisite." (*People* identified it as a 3.27-carat, square-shaped, emerald-cut ring that would retail for $60,000.) Though Paula cut out photos from magazines and left a few around the apartment for her boyfriend, a twenty-nine-year-old stockbroker, to find, she was still pleasantly surprised by the nearly three-carat ring she got.

"I love my ring. It's really perfect, and I felt so fortunate to get such a beautiful one," she says. "My friends went nuts for my ring, too. It's adorable—even a year later, they beg me to try it on! They can't believe how ornate it is and they love the weight of it."

Of course, Paula isn't the only one of her friends with a big engagement ring. "I have definitely noticed larger engagement rings as a major trend," she says. "A few years ago, I would have thought a carat to a carat and a half was generous. But recently, they've gotten so much more opulent. I knew that when I got engaged, I wanted two carats."

Paula says her ring is "quite sizably larger" than her mother's or her grandmother's, but part of that was a perk of getting engaged in financial boom times. A few months after her wedding, when the recession hit, she said, "Everyone should be more cognizant of their big spending. I know in retrospect, I would have been."

The message of Tiffany's, according to a 2007 article in *The New York Times,* is "bring on the bling." That made sense in 2007 and the two decades leading up to it, when a supersized rock would match a supersized SUV and McMansion. During the 2008–2009 recession, Tiffany's business in the United States dropped by about a quarter. That was due in large part to fewer sales in the $10,000 engagement ring range, from middle-of-the-road buyers who didn't usually shop at places like Tiffany's but were onetime splurging. International tourists were still buying at the Tiffany flagship, says Mr. R. Two foreign couples, one pair from Japan and another from Russia, bought rings while I was browsing, causing the sales associates to bring out flutes of champagne for them. And even during the recession, Tiffany's had no trouble selling its $50,000-and-up engagement rings. It seemed that 2008 hit the reset button, returning the store to its original place as a jewelry provider not to the middle-class masses but to the überelite.

Still, the recession wasn't easy on jewelers. Signet Jewelers Ltd., the world's largest jewelry store owner, posted a $424 million loss in 2009. Tiffany's posted a 76 percent drop in net income. According to watchmaker Movado, about 15 percent of U.S. jewelry stores closed from 2008 to 2009. Zales, the biggest U.S. jewelry chain, announced in 2009 it would shutter 115 stores.

I ask Mr. R if he thinks the recession might mark the end of the two-carat diamond's reign.

"Never," he says. "A recession is a phase, but a diamond is forever."

6.
SHOPPING INSIDE THE BOX

Today is Wish Day, when an eighteen-year-old boy named De-Shawn will walk around this generic, suburban, big-box store and buy a lot of stuff, courtesy of the Make-A-Wish Foundation. Wish Day for DeShawn is a lot like any other Saturday in the suburbs, people busily buzzing around, filling their carts with stuff to take home.

When DeShawn was first diagnosed with Hodgkin's disease, his family found diversion in shopping. DeShawn spent most of the money from his summer job downloading songs online. His mom bought DeShawn new shirts and shoes, so even though he was losing weight, he'd still have clothes that fit. Sure, the stuff they bought didn't change the fact that DeShawn's cancer was already in stage IIIB, the last stage before the final—and almost always terminal—stage IV, in which the cancer spreads to the bone marrow. DeShawn goes to the local children's hospital three days a week for rounds of radiation and chemo, plugged into the drip of toxic chemicals that poison him, make him weak, bald, and puffy. And no, shopping doesn't change how uncomfortable it is to have that port, that plastic-ringed hole, in his chest. But he does have $3,000 in cash from the Make-A-Wish Foundation to spend on anything he wants, any*where* he wants—and he wants to spend it all at this big-box store.

Make-A-Wish also provides a limo, which dropped off DeShawn

and his family right in front of the giant, automatic sliding doors this morning. I drive separately, pulling into the parking lot with the big-box store on the end. Since it is a rainy Saturday at a suburban strip mall, the massive lot is full for the first several rows, so I pull into a spot in the far reaches, almost in the corner. I grumble and pull out my umbrella and book it the fifty yards or so to the store. It turns out that I'm not alone in my grumbling—the size of the parking lot is people's number one complaint about big-box stores, that it takes them too long to get inside. In fact, "No other landmass uses more pavement than big-box stores because they require such large parking lots. The parking lot is typically three or four times larger than the actual store," says Stacy Mitchell. I'd called her because she's the author of *Big-Box Swindle: The True Cost of Mega-Retailers and the Fight for America's Independent Businesses*. In addition to developing land, parking lots wreak havoc on the environment because "polluted storm water runoff from parking lots is now a threat to bodies of water like lakes and rivers all over the country. All of the oils that accumulate on the parking lot from your car get washed off in a torrent to the nearest stream. In a lot of regions, pavement is now one of the bigger pollution problems for rivers," says Mitchell.

It's a shock to the system going from the air outside—humid and smelling of worms from the rain—to the blast of sterile, freezing air-conditioning beyond the sliding doors. The gray indoor-outdoor carpeting is tracked with wet footprints. Staff zip around DeShawn as he walks through the aisles of cameras and M&M-printed mouse pads and flat-screen televisions. I'm here, my sneakers squishing and squeaking, because DeShawn and his family agreed to let me follow him around today. But he's so timid he won't make eye contact with me for more than a moment at a time, and when he answers my questions he looks down at his boots. He's shy. He's a boy who has a swarm of parents, Make-A-Wish volunteers, and the store's staff in their polo shirts—and me—all hovering around him, watching to see what he buys.

I'm standing here with DeShawn's whole family, all of us wearing matching Make-A-Wish T-shirts. There's Jihan, DeShawn's nine-year-old sister, who wears earrings that are little white Js. Tenisha, his mom, has on a batik-dyed scarf and her hair wrapped into little tiny braids at the top and loose at the bottom. Jim, his dad, wears a ski cap and Iverson sneakers and a big diamond earring, which DeShawn also wears, but a scaled-down version. DeShawn has his Make-A-Wish shirt under a matching pale blue suede tracksuit and tan construction boots so new and smooth that they resemble the contour of his head. Mine is XXL and hangs over my jeans like I'm a little kid playing dress up. I'm learning it's much harder to feel like a real reporter in a gigantic starchy T-shirt.

We're here, in a big-box store, because this is where money goes far. About 12 percent of the entire U.S. economy's gains in the late 1990s could be traced to Walmart alone. For the most part, DeShawn's parents also fit the profile of the typical big-box consumer: between the ages of twenty-five and forty-nine, likely to live in the South or Midwest, with an annual income below $75,000.

Shopping in big stores owned by big companies is nothing new. Walmart's been around since 1962, but it was the 1920s and '30s when companies like grocery store chain the Great Atlantic & Pacific Tea Company (A&P) first dominated the market, running five times the number of stores Walmart has today. These days only five hundred or so A&P stores exist—compared to 16,000 in its heyday.

* * *

Of all the big-box stores, Walmart reigns: it is the world's largest retailer. "Clearly, Walmart is more powerful than any retailer has ever been," says Edward Fox, head of Southern Methodist University's JCPenney Center for Retailing Excellence. According to Charles Fishman, author of *The Walmart Effect,* that company has "shaped the U.S. economy more than any institution except for the federal government." Walmart accounts for between 8 and 10 percent of *all* retail spending in the country, which is extraordinary for a single institution. But that doesn't even begin to get at the reality of its scope until you look at individual sectors. For example, Walmart accounts for 20 percent of all grocery spending in the country, and for 30 or 40 percent of it in places like Memphis, Dallas-Fort Worth, and Oklahoma City. Walmart accounts for 20 to 25 percent of all toy spending in America. They get 25 percent of all health and beauty spending on stuff like shampoo and toothpaste. Fishman's responses to my questions were consistently shocking.

"Walmart sells more toys than Toys 'R' Us," he says. "Walmart sells more electronics than Circuit City—that's why Circuit City went out of business. Walmart sells more blue jeans of its own brand than Levi Strauss does of its brand."

There are now approximately 4,000 Walmarts in America and 3,000 abroad. Sixty-two percent of Americans live within five miles of a Walmart, and a staggering 94 percent of Americans live within fifteen miles of one (that number would shoot up dramatically, notes Fishman, if a Walmart were put in Times Square, the Loop in Chicago, and downtown L.A., where there currently are none). At this point, 140 million Americans shop at Walmart each week. That's more than half of the adults in America, more than the number of people who voted for Barack Obama and John McCain combined. Walmart's 2009 numbers reflect almost $406 billion in sales, around $1.1 billion in business every day. Walmart no longer has any real rivals. It does more business than Target, Sears, Kmart, JCPenney, Safeway, and Kroger combined.

The result of that massive, mind-numbing size, of course, is unrivaled power. For many companies who do business with Walmart, Walmart is not only their biggest customer but is bigger than the next five or ten customers combined—so Walmart gets to throw its (extremely substantial) weight around. "That means dictating not only the price, but what kind of products are available, how they're packaged, the quantity, where they're made, who they're made by, what they look like, what colors they come in, and their level of quality," says Fishman.

That also means Walmart can make crushing demands on suppliers, like demanding they reduce the product price by 5 percent every year. Eventually, that means the supplier needs to take drastic measures to meet the price demand, which often translates to shuttering a U.S. factory and sending the business to Mexico or China, where the labor is cheaper. Companies that don't want to take their production out of the United States risk getting dropped, because Walmart is more concerned about profit margins than loyalty; they will simply buy the product from someone else who is willing to sell them that product at the lower price. This leaves American businesses in a catch-22: either their U.S. factory closes because they have to move the work to Mexico or China just to stay in the game, or their U.S. factory closes because Walmart pulls their business, so they lose their biggest buyer by ten times. Walmart has immense power over consumer product companies. To stay in business yourself, you essentially must do business with them. In this sense, the reason so many American companies are shipping their work overseas is because of one supersized American company.

DeShawn drags his feet on the never-ending industrial gray carpet, clearly tired of waiting for his family to catch up to him. Since he was diagnosed with lymphoma, his life, to put it plainly, has sucked. He has to stay home from school for the rest of the year, spending most of his time in his bedroom. No more riding his bike with his friends; no more shooting hoops.

DeShawn's family still hasn't noticed his impatience, his itchiness to get shopping. So he walks over to a game system plugged into a giant TV, stands there tapping the colored buttons on the controller, bleep-bloops and gun-loading noises burping from the speakers. He gets a dopey smile on his face, and his tongue pokes out to the side of his mouth in concentration, Michael Jordan-like, as he hunts bad guys. He puts down the controller and stares at the video game boxes locked away behind a Plexiglas case. I can't stop looking at his face, his expression of pure joy and anticipation. In my mind, I watch him turn from a quiet, shy boy who doesn't seem to care about much into a boy who is contemplating the plausibility of shattering Plexiglas with his fist so he can get to the games. It's that rush of knowing that everything he's seeing could be his. It's a glorious intoxication that takes over every cell. Never for one tiny moment do you think you'll stop feeling like this. This feeling, I remember, is what big-box shopping can be about. There's something exhilarating about knowing you could have anything you wanted in the whole place. It's a feeling most of us can't afford to have in a boutique, but it's one lots of us can have walking into a big-box store.

* * *

When some people think of American businesses like Walmart, they may think of American ingenuity. After all, we invented game-changers like the Industrial Revolution–inspiring factory assembly line. But for others, American business brings to mind corporate greed, scammers from Enron to Freddie Mac.

On a 2009 *Forbes* list of the world's biggest companies, nine of the top twenty-five were American, a blowout considering the next highest countries were China and the United Kingdom, tied with three apiece. And why not? The unofficial mantra of American businesses had been "grow, baby, grow" for years. The Bush administration, for example, maintained a laissez-faire approach to busting up potential monopolies. A 2009 *New York Times* blog called "High-Tech Antitrust Cases: The Road Ahead" summarized the Bush administration's approach this way: "Big companies are agents of economic efficiency that should be constrained only if their behavior 'disproportionately harms consumers.'" Obama's pick for Justice Department's chief antitrust economist, Carl Shapiro, wrote in 2008 that approximately thirty business-expanding mergers or buyouts that would've historically been challenged weren't touched under Bush, citing big-money mergers like Whirlpool and Maytag or Sirius XM.

Though an emphasis on big business may be a more recent development in America's history, it's still an undeniably American concept. Before the Civil War and through the middle of the nineteenth century, American businesses that were considered big were usually single-plantation or single-factory firms. "There weren't even that many of them," says Gene Smiley, professor emeritus of economics at Marquette University. "And American firms weren't that much bigger than businesses in Germany or Britain."

All of that changed, however, over the next fifty years. The mid-
to late-nineteenth century saw the rise of big businesses similar to
what we think of today. That was possible, says Smiley, due to
three crucial factors: development of rapid, relatively cheap transportation (refrigeration advancements, steamships, and a railroad
system for shipping across the country); development of commu-
nication (telegraphs, which allowed for multi-site firms to work
together); and finally, Wall Street's stock exchanges, which meant
the beginnings of a sophisticated financial network that let corpo-
rations attract capital from investors who weren't part of the man-
aging family. Before that, nearly all big businesses were family-run
empires (think Rockefeller or Carnegie), but the end of the nineteenth century brought more familiar-looking companies, owned
by shareholders, with a board of directors and a CEO.

Those companies thrived in America because, as Smiley says,
"due to our physical size and population size, we had a very large
market and the ability to bring about large, large firms to operate
in that market." There was also a huge merger wave from 1890 to
1902 that resulted in ever-larger companies still.

But why, in such a relatively young country, did big business take
off in a way it didn't in other parts of the world? "In many ways, we
were the most progressive country on earth. By the beginning of
the twentieth century, we clearly had the highest incomes, by far,
and the most entrepreneurial companies in the world," says Smiley.
Perhaps the most important reason why big business didn't spread
in Europe was how fragmented Europe was, with "tariff barriers,
differences in currency, and differences in taxation, which limited
the size of the markets that a lot of those firms could operate in.
You could move products across states in America and be operating under the same rules, the same currency, but try moving some-

thing in Europe over the same distance, and it's one small country to another, which means a whole new set of regulations. That's a barrier to creating a big market. That's what they've basically tried to undo with the European Union and the euro, while this whole time we've had a huge area that allows for a common market."

Large, unified countries like Canada couldn't match America's soaring businesses, either; Canada's population was much smaller and more spread out. By 1902, America began to see the formation of what would become its iconic companies, from Carnegie Steel to the Standard Oil Corporation and General Electric.

GE was one of the original dozen companies on the Dow, and the only one that remains today. It was founded in 1878 by Thomas Edison. It has huge international reach as the fourth most-recognized brand in the world. In 2006, *Fortune* named GE America's Most Admired Company. You could practically see the stars and stripes waving behind those two iconic cursive letters.

But by March 2009, *The Washington Post* reported that the "battered" company, whose stock prices slid to lows not seen since 1992, required "massive additional assistance from the U.S. government." The article, called "Faltering Giants: Corporate America's Icons Crumbling Under Global Recession," went on to say that "while GE's fate might indeed mirror the nation's for now, the company could perish before an economic recovery arrives."

Clearly, GE is in a precarious position indeed. On one hand, it doesn't seem surprising: the recession pistol-whipped companies of all sizes. On the other hand, it's alarming that a company so huge, so storied, large enough to amass such diversified assets—everything from TV shows to lightbulbs—could be so hard hit; it seems as though the company's sheer size should insulate it, at least to a considerable degree, against folding. But the ultimate surprise is that companies like GE aren't failing in spite of their size, but *because* of it. The article pointed to companies like GE as well as Citigroup, Kraft Foods, and General Motors, saying: "The girth that once seemed a source of strength now appears to be undermining them."

Some of what we think of as the largest companies in America—Bank of America, McDonald's—are really just smaller businesses under one umbrella of management, like the bank's various branches or the restaurant's individual franchises. But a significant part of why size worked against large companies is that, due to their size, they could do their own financing. That means certain large companies could lend money to their own customers. And if you're deciding if your customer can get money to buy *your* product, you're probably not going to be the most objective judge of whether they're truly a sound loan candidate. It basically means these companies stood to make money on both ends of the deal—they'd make money when they lent to consumers who would spend it on their products, and they'd make money off interest when the customer was repaying the loan. *The Washington Post* said that, "when the credit markets ground to a halt in mid-September, it set off a chain reaction of pain, hurting consumers and manufacturers alike." Supersized companies that include consumers and manufacturers were then doubly hurt, since consumers were no longer buying as much of the companies' products and were often unable to repay their loans.

But another *Washington Post* article says that hands-off big-business policy is changing under President Obama. It reported that Obama's Department of Justice would investigate constantly expanding technology networks, specifically the likes of Google and Microsoft. Christine Varney, Obama's Assistant Attorney

General to the Department of Justice for the Antitrust Division, will be a "a much tougher cop than her predecessor" at busting up dangerously large companies, according to *Fortune*. In fact, she said at a 2008 panel for the American Antitrust Institute that the U.S. economy will "continually see a problem, potentially with Google," saying the company "acquired a monopoly in Internet online advertising." That may have come as an unpleasant surprise to Google CEO Eric Schmidt, who told the BBC in 2009 that the United States should break up banks that get "too big to fail," raising eyebrows about whether people in glass Googleplexes should be throwing stones. Debate carries on about whether Varney will actually pursue Google, with *Fortune* reporting that, "Prognosticators aren't certain whether she'll actually choose to go after Google."

Either way, old-school GE and new-wave Google—and all the giant companies in between—raise an important question: are supersized businesses good for America? In some ways, of course, they are. They make big money. They provide jobs for millions of Americans. They can offer more services or sell more products in more parts of the country. Thanks to economy of scale—the sheer volume of what a company can do in terms of manufacturing and distribution—big companies can produce or distribute their products at a lower cost, which often means lower costs for consumers (hello, Target, Walmart, and Costco trifecta).

But as we've seen, big companies don't weather economic downturns much better than smaller companies.

"Take automobile companies in the Great Depression," Smiley says. "A lot of the smaller companies that had been marginally viable simply had to close their doors or lay off something like 60 to 70 percent of their employees, like the Nash Motor Car Company. Some companies survived, like Ford, but that was less due to its size and more due to excellent management. I'm not sure the large firms weathered the Depression any better than the small firms did, since it wiped out both. So bigness wasn't necessarily a thing that could save a company. It's the same thing for the current recession—if a big company survives, it's because of its management, not its size," he says. "Size can't save you."

The Make-A-Wish volunteer entourage walks a few steps behind DeShawn. They greeted him at the front door of the big-box store this morning, holding homemade, sparkly "Welcome, DeShawn!!!" posters, adorned with lots of exclamation points. Wish Day is absolutely teeming with exclamation, even if its recipient is more subdued.

But DeShawn does love music (enough to merit a fraction of an exclamation point, perhaps). He decides to spend more than half of his money on a high-tech piano keyboard, so he can make his own hip-hop beats. The big-box store cuts Make-A-Wish a break and gives DeShawn the $2,400 keyboard for $1,599.99, so now he has a lot of money left over to spend. He has exactly $1,400.01. I know this because it's written in pencil on a small piece of scrap paper DeShawn is carrying around, balled up in his hand. He insists on writing it all out instead of using a calculator, a curious choice for a teenage technophile.

Tenisha, his mom, is surprised, too, because usually all of the needles pricking DeShawn's arm make it difficult for him to hold on to a pen.

When I first met him, he reminded me of a basketball player: tall, hands big but soft-looking, arms so wide they should be called a wingspan. DeShawn's skin is smooth and even, and his voice is the exact same way. His head is bald from the chemo, contributing to the basketball star look, but there is no stubble like when you're just shaving your head.

As we approach the glistening wall of TVs, I want to ask DeShawn: if you were allowed one wish, anything, truly without limit, what would it be? I doubt it would be a trip to Disney World, or a computer, or a television, not anything on the Make-A-Wish Foundation's form. I imagine he would wish to be better, healthy, like normal kids who don't know any better, shooting hoops at the playground, picking out a tuxedo to wear to the prom, riding his bike down the street so fast that the wind whips his long eyelashes like willow branches.

Big-box stores like Walmart, with their low prices and seemingly infinite selection, might seem like they'd have universal appeal. But while American stores have thrived, the chain recently had to close stores in Germany and South Korea, where locals supposedly couldn't get over the idea of why you'd ever need to buy so much, especially at once. But in America, big-box stores keep growing, if not in terms of popularity, at least in where we spend our money. A 2006 list compiled by *Stores* magazine showed that of the top ten biggest retailers, five were "low-priced, big-box chains," including Walmart, Target, and Costco (compared to only two out of ten in the 1990s, when Target and Costco didn't make the list). Walmart alone opens between 170 and 270 new stores every year, adding at least 20 million square feet of retail space to their company's ownership.

Walmart is so easy to focus on because it's dramatically dominant over the other big boxes. Walmart sells by St. Patrick's Day what number two retailer Home Depot or number three retailer Target sells for the whole year. If you've been in all three of these stores, and you probably have, you'll already know that each has its own feel; if someone walked you in blindfolded, you'd still likely know if you were in a Target or a Walmart.

"Walmart is a place to buy stuff; Target is a place to shop," says author Charles Fishman. "At Target, the shelves don't come up as high, and you feel like you can breathe. Walmart's goal is simple: to put as much merchandise as possible in every square foot of store space." That's because the more they put out, the more they sell. So if you are in an aisle of Walmart, the shelves are a foot or two above your head. You can't see anywhere else in the store. You are in the canyons of Walmart. You can't get your cart through the racks of apparel without knocking something over.

If you're not running around the store with thousands of dollars to spend, as DeShawn is, the experience of shopping at a big-box store can be unpleasantly overwhelming. So why do we keep shopping there? The main reason is that it's significantly cheaper. "Walmart sells groceries on average for 15 percent less than the other major national chains—not for generic or house brands but for the same brand-name stuff," says Fishman. It's true; essentially, 80 percent of the stuff in Target and Walmart is exactly the same, but Walmart can sell the same things for 10 percent, 15 percent, even 20 percent cheaper. "So you're saving 15 percent just by parking your car in their parking lot." And that 15 percent on everything from milk to a big-screen TV can add up to a huge difference. Considering the average family income in America is $55,000 a year, "saving 15 percent on groceries equals out to almost eight weeks of groceries for free a year. Why would you even hesitate? For a lot of folks, that's a huge difference. You could now go on a vacation that you couldn't otherwise afford, or send your kids to sleepaway camp," says Fishman. For DeShawn, that means his $3,000 go 15 percent further, basically giving him an extra $450 to spend. When the numbers are broken down that way, for a lot of people, big-box stores are hard to argue against. But those savings come at a cost—a cost that is ultimately passed down to American workers, companies, and communities. "The price issue is really questionable when you look at how much we've given up in terms of income and opportunity," says Stacy Mitchell, author of *Big-Box Swindle*. "The question is, are we really better off at the end of the day? I would argue that we're worse off financially."

The other important reason people shop at big-box stores is convenience. "There isn't an area of retail in which Walmart doesn't do business. They are the country's second-largest pharmacy, so you put your prescription in, do some shopping, and pick it up on the way to the checkout. They do car oil changes. You can buy jeans and a fish tank and a bra and a sleeping bag and a DVD all at the same place," says Fishman. "These days you can do that at a lot of big-box stores, but Walmart was really the first to make sure you could get whatever you needed in one stop." Plus, most shoppers are visually cued—meaning, you come in for a closet organizer and walk by a display of laundry detergent and remember, "Hey, we need laundry detergent," and pick some up. "When you sell everything, there is a chance that someone will buy something that they didn't know that they needed," Fishman says. "It's convenient for customers, but it also means the store picks up business it wouldn't otherwise get."

Though DeShawn is mostly spending his money on electronics-related items, he still can do it all in one place by going to a big-box store. He doesn't have to go to a music shop for a keyboard, and an electronics shop, and a video game shop. It's all right here, and it's all cheap.

I watch DeShawn slowly weave through the aisles, running his fingers over a keyboard or clicking a mouse or turning a dial. The beeps and taps and rounds of machine-gun fire blasting from the rows of televisions don't appear to bother him. He seems calmed by all the stuff, a calm I think I recognize, available for purchase. DeShawn picks up a remote and points it at one of the TVs, flipping it from a basketball game to *Scarface*. He looks down at the remote and smiles for a second.

Here in the sensory overload of a big-box store, time comes in flashes. DeShawn's next to me, then zipping over there. First there's a Disney movie on the giant TV, then sports, then an action movie. There's certainly no time to get bored, but there's also not much time to think, and maybe that's exactly why this form of shopping is the perfect distraction. Accumulating stuff, especially in big-box stores, is difficult: there are so many choices for a buyer like DeShawn to make, numbers to deal with, sounds for your brain to filter out. There's no time to think about what a $3,000 shopping spree means, or what cancer means. In this sensory overload, it's hard enough to pick out what you want, put it in your cart, and pay for it. That's why shopping in a big-box store is such a comfort—the experience makes it hard to focus on anything else.

Right now, DeShawn seems like someone who's happy to shop as he cruises past the rows of computers. I remember how he told me he was diagnosed. He felt a lump in his groin. He knew something wasn't right. So he went to where he always felt most comfortable, the computer. He searched and searched, reading everything he could find about what this lump could be. He told his mother, Teni-sha, who is a nurse. She made a doctor's appointment; she knew it didn't sound good. Not even three weeks after DeShawn first noticed something that felt a little weird, they told him. Cancer. Lymphoma. Hodgkin's. The family cried for what felt like forever. DeShawn, for his part, was mad. I can't imagine this quiet, almost somber kid being mad. But Tenisha tells me that while the rest of them cried, DeShawn got pissed off—yelling, swearing, punching the air.

DeShawn has already picked out a new Wish Day computer. His scrunched-up note now says $704 left. He makes a beeline across the store. When I catch up to him, he's standing in front of a wall of stereos. His current stereo is a portable CD player that he hooked up to some speakers; the one he's looking at now, awe-struck, has a five-CD changer, subwoofers, and six speakers. It's black and red, with silver geometric spokes covering the speakers that look like rims in a Snoop Dogg video. A big-box store em-ployee throws in a demo CD, and the sound comes out so clear it's as though you can feel it prick the individual hairs on the inside of your ears. DeShawn stands right in front of the speaker, looking up at it and smiling.

"He plays his music too loud already," says Jim, his dad. "With this thing, the neighbors'll be calling as soon as we go out."

Tenisha shoots her husband a shushing look. "Today is *DeShawn's day*," she says, but DeShawn doesn't say anything.

He looks at the price tag on the shelf, the neatly typed numbers. He repeats them in shaky pencil below the $704 and does some subtraction. He writes $464 and draws a little circle around it.

Today, on Wish Day, Tenisha, Jim, and Jihan, along with the Make-A-Wish volunteers, seem to be trying to erase his pain with an extravagant dance of happiness. Their tones are exaggerated as they ooh and aah over his purchases, their voices forcefully inflating the room with joy. It's as if stuff alone is not enough, like they need to admire the stuff to give DeShawn bonus happiness points. The music is still pumping from the stereo, so loud people several aisles away are turning around to stare. I give them a curt smile, starting to feel protective of DeShawn myself.

Shopping at big-box stores that replace mom-and-pop shops may have consequences that go unconsidered, such as contributing to environmental damage and pollution. "Shopping-related driving has shot up more than 40 percent since 1990," says Mitchell. "At first, I thought it was just suburban sprawl. But driving for shopping purposes has grown three times more than for any other purpose, like commuting to work. We take about the same number of trips as we used to. If you think about the geography, in a city or a region that had twelve hardware stores that were scattered across many neighborhoods, now there is just this one big Home Depot. So now everyone in that region has to drive a little bit farther to pick up a gallon of paint or a hammer. You end up with these big regional stores as opposed to smaller business that provided goods and services in walking distance or a short ride from the house."

Another result of big-box stores is the rise of the disposable culture. Before there were supercheap superstores, you bought an item like a lawn mower, and when it broke, you brought it back to the shop where you bought it or to a machine repair shop and you got it fixed.

"The Walmart effect is that you can buy a lawn mower for $109, less than you might pay for a neighborhood kid to mow your lawn four times, and you use it for a year," says Fishman. "The only problem with that is, after you store it over the winter and take it out the next April, it probably won't start. If you can even find a place to get it repaired, that will probably cost almost $109, so you just put the old lawn mower on the curb and drive to Walmart and buy a new one."

Even if nothing from the big-box stores lasts, it's cheap enough that it doesn't have to.

DeShawn is, in Make-A-Wish parlance, an "I wish to have." A couple of weeks ago, his nurse told him about the Make-A-Wish Foundation. She said they grant wishes, almost whatever you want, to kids with life-threatening medical conditions. Make-A-Wish has been around since 1980 and has granted 110,000 wishes, all different kinds of ways to offer a little relief.

Make-A-Wish offers a few options: I wish to be (a day as a fireman, a police officer, or a model, for example); I wish to meet (a favorite athlete, musician, TV or movie star); I wish to go (travel to a theme park, exotic beach, cruise, sporting event or concert), and I wish to have, for kids who "wish for a special gift, like a computer, a tree house, a shopping spree, or something that they have coveted for a long time."

DeShawn was thinking "I wish to go," a trip to Hawaii, with beaches and oceans and sun and those fluorescent drinks with paper umbrellas in them. So his mom called Make-A-Wish to make sure he could do something besides go to Disney World. Trips to Disney World are the most popular request, garnering 45 percent of all wishes, followed by gifts or shopping sprees, at 30 percent. Make-A-Wish said DeShawn could do or have almost anything, could go almost anywhere, could meet almost anyone. But like lots of us, he wanted stuff. And so he went to a big-box store, a place to spend $3,000 in two hours.

Trailing behind DeShawn as he passes the computers for the second time, their screens a virtual aquarium of under-the-sea screen savers, I want to know how he got from "I want to go" to "I want to have." I want to know how so many of us, really, end up this way.

He told me he looked around his room, which he'd started to regard as his prison of boredom. He dreamed about turning the place into an entertainment center, about buying TVs and computers and stereos and DVD players to keep himself entertained. He would blast the boredom away with wires and amps and electricity, all of the things he wanted to buy but his parents couldn't quite afford now. Then Make-A-Wish told him he could have $3,000 to redeem at a big-box store.

He spent weeks online, comparing prices and brands and megapixels. Right now, with a television remote in his hand and his eyes glassy as he stares at Pacino's HD face on plasma, DeShawn doesn't seem like he's worried about what his gift wish means. He doesn't seem to be thinking about the fact that he has a lump in his groin or a port in his side, that when Wish Day is over, he'll be left with those things, plus a pile of wires and screens.

When a big-box store moves in, what might seem like a boon to the community can often be anything but, Mitchell tells me—though many cities welcome these stores because they seem like economic development, since they provide new jobs. But data shows it's not really growth. Studies done at the University of California, Irvine, found that a new Walmart doesn't actually create new jobs. In fact, it actually destroys jobs. For every one job at a Walmart store, about 1.4 existing jobs are lost. That's simply because Walmart does the same amount of business with fewer employees. Plus, the jobs it does "create" are low-wage jobs. Walmart's business model basically keeps the working poor at their current economic station.

In addition, "a new big-box store doesn't mean that more people are going to buy paper towels or CDs. It just means that money going into that big-box's cash registers is coming out of cash registers someplace else," says Mitchell, like out of local businesses that are forced to close when they have to compete against a big-box's prices or hours, yet another economic impact. When a big-box store comes in, communities tend to lose a lot of locally owned businesses. Local businesses tend to spend the money they make on other local businesses; they get their printing done locally, they hire a local accountant. A big-box retailer doesn't have the need for local goods and services, so the money that goes into their stores just leaves the local economy. Much of their business is now being outsourced to other countries, so you don't even get those dollars circulating in the national economy.

But there are much greater consequences than just financial ones. "Due to the way we experience where we live, communities that are dominated by a few big businesses, compared to communities that have mostly small businesses, show a striking difference in measures of social and civic health," says Mitchell. "Even when the studies control for education and other important factors, the small-business communities, all else being equal, have higher median incomes, less income inequality, and lower infant mortality rates. Many more people belong to a neighborhood organization, community group, or civic cause. They also go to city council and school board meetings much more frequently, and they even vote more often than people who live in big-business communities." In addition, the number one reason we leave home, aside from going to work, is to run an errand. "Walking around the business district, saying hello to a shop owner or running into someone you know—it's building social capital, a feeling of being connected to your community," says Mitchell. The farther you have to drive from home to do that, the less chance there is that you'll run into someone you know. "The number of conversations that people have with other customers in big stores is much fewer than what you see on Main Street, or at the farmer's market, or any other small-scale community shopping experience. At those regional big-box stores, you don't get the sense of connection and camaraderie, the way communities share information that gives people a stake in the place that they live."

Not surprisingly, then, some communities want big-box stores gone. A city council in Kauai, Hawaii, passed a 2007 ordinance prohibiting development of any retail or wholesale establishment bigger than 75,000 square feet, a direct response to a local Walmart's plan to expand to 185,00 square feet. The San Diego City Council passed a similar ban in 2007, only for it to be vetoed by Mayor Jerry Sanders; near-identical legislation has been introduced in other parts of California and Washington state; Washington, D.C.; Austin, Texas; and Chicago, Illinois as well.

In a few parts of the country, these altars of big, cheap consumerism are struggling, like Kmart and Circuit City, which both went bankrupt. In the town of Sterling Heights, Michigan, a complex that used to house a Home Quarters and a Kmart was revamped. In 2008, the Grace Christian Church spent $15 million to renovate the old space into a megachurch with "an 1,800-seat sanctuary, a 400-seat children's church and 400-seat youth church, a basketball court, and a 200-seat café and coffee bar with wireless Internet capability."

But perhaps the most intimidating thing about big-box stores isn't their size—it's the fact that they've completely altered the shopping and economic landscapes to the point where stores like Walmart are inescapable.

"Ultimately, it doesn't matter where you shop," says Fishman. "Maybe you refuse to shop at Walmart because you don't like their business practices and you don't want to give them your money. But wherever you *do* shop, at a Best Buy, Kohl's, or a local business, that store is competing with Walmart, which means you are still getting the benefit of Walmart. Merchants and businesspeople around the country that are close to a Walmart have no choice but to live in the Walmart economy. Walmart sells more bikes than anywhere else in the country. That means if the local bicycle shop wants to sell you a bike, they have to think about how to sell compared with Walmart. If they try to compete on price, they lose—Walmart will always be able to sell you a cheaper bike. If they try to compete on convenience, they lose—Walmart is open twenty-four hours and so can sell you a bike at 1:00 A.M. To succeed, a business has to overcome all of Walmart's advantages in price and convenience." And it's not just for bikes, of course. Walmart sells more eye makeup than anybody, more cigarettes than anybody, more movies than anybody. "That means if you're a competitor selling pretty much any type of product, you're thinking about one thing, and that's Walmart."

While Jim and Tenisha remind everyone around that it's DeShawn's day, that it's all for him and making him happy, DeShawn doesn't seem so happy anymore. He's been milling around the store, picking things out and having the store employee stack them in the cart, and he's almost out of money. Now DeShawn is the least animated of the bunch, walking through the store nearly silent, shadowlike, not at all jovial and spastic like those contestants on *Supermarket Sweep*. As we wind down on Wish Day, he seems resigned.

DeShawn finishes doing the subtraction and adds the scrap piece of paper to the stack of printouts he brought to the store with photos, prices, and brands of all the products he'd been researching. He picks out the video game system I saw him play before, a chunk of plastic that costs him $300. When he looks at it in his cart, there's no longer even half of a smile. DeShawn has one more thing on his list, an MP3 player, which he picks out in under two minutes with his remaining $164. He does a few more subtractions. Now he's ready to check out. He's spent his $3,000 down to eleven cents, a feat that would win him a prize on many game shows, and garners more oohs and aahs from the volunteers.

DeShawn seems uncomfortable with all this attention, like if he can just stare at the carpet for long enough, we'll all forget he's here and we'll wander off to do something else.

One of the Make-A-Wish volunteers hands DeShawn the money in hundred dollar bills to pay for his purchases. First, DeShawn poses for a photo with the bills fanned out near his face, right next to his diamond earring. All that green and white truly is startling to see in real life—this much cash is usually reserved for mafia movies or rap videos or briefcases lined in red velvet, and we all need a minute to soak it all in before DeShawn hands it over to the cashier with a sigh. I wonder if we're all imagining the same thing: think how much stuff you could get with that.

The rain's dried up, leaving the air a hot, thick gray. I watch the family load their boxes into the limo, packages on top of packages.

DeShawn still seems resigned. He looks at the boxes and back at his list, eleven cents, before crushing it up and stuffing it in his pocket.

As the Make-A-Wish volunteers take some family photos, Jihan, the little sister, is in her glory. In front of the camera, her smile shows various stages of baby and adult teeth. In the vast expanse of parking lot, the family stands around the limo and waits for a copy of the photo from the store's digital camera and inkjet printer. The limo driver seems to know what this brother-sister rivalry is all about, and he nudges DeShawn. He thinks no one else can hear him, but I do.

"How about we make Ms. America here clean the limo?" the driver says. "We can make her wash the windows, soap up the car, whaddya think?"

And DeShawn laughs out loud, for the first time today.

7.

THE NEW BARBIE DREAM CAR

When I meet Robert, the Hummer salesman, I wish for a moment I had long acrylic nails, perfectly French manicured, rather than my bitten-down ones, nails that still show a bit of neuroses, which I like to translate to societal awareness/guilt/concern. Someone buying a Hummer, I hope, has none of that neurotic awareness and guilt and concern left, or never had any to begin with. Because I'm terrified here that I'm not as far from them as I want to be, as I used to be. I need to know how close I really am to whom I used to consider the enemy.

Robert is the salesman who will later tell me to put a picture of myself driving the Hummer on my parents' refrigerator, because then my daddy will buy it for me. "Works every time," he says. "Once you imagine yourself in it, act like you already own it, it's as good as yours.

"Also, start saying '*my* Hummer,'" he recommends.

I'm walking between rows of hulking metal behind Robert, trying not to hit my head on the side-view mirrors as we walk to the Hummer we're going to test-drive. I'm here, at this never-ending parking lot of H2s, the second generation of Hummers, because I need to know if I could own one. Not in terms of the price tag, but in terms of conscience. On one hand, I think Hummers are a waste, a giant, gas- and oil-guzzling, too-damn-big-for-its-own-good waste. On the other hand, before I moved to New York City and could easily go car-free, I spent many years happily driving a Jeep. My father and my brother both drive SUVs. Yes, I knew driving an SUV wasn't the best choice for the environment and that the vehicle parked in front of my house helped fuel wars in the Middle East. But it was also . . . convenient.

I wonder if all SUVs might be gateway drugs to hard-core SUVs, the Escalades and the Sequoias and the mother lode, the Hummer. I wonder that if I hadn't given up the Jeep and moved to a mostly car-ownership-free zone, maybe I would've eventually traded in my Jeep for an even bigger SUV. So I've come to try to figure out who this salesman and this company think the Hummer people are. Are they people who started with smaller SUVs and just keep upsizing? Are they people with McMansions, who worship at megachurches, who need a car whose scale matches the sheer size of everything else in their lives? Or are they like me— people just looking for convenience, a little luxury?

I wonder how the Hummer people justify buying a car so big. Are they using the same line as me: it's just more convenient? Do they still donate to the World Wildlife Fund and the Sierra Club, like I do, a tithe of guilt? Or have they found a way to stop being consumed by guilt, to just enjoy getting what they want? If parking spaces are getting fewer and smaller, and emissions laws are getting tighter, and jobs are getting outsourced, and gas prices are getting higher, and the Arctic temperature is going up from global warming, then why does our dream car keep getting bigger? I can't tell if it's a willful turning away from the world's problems and pretending they don't exist, or thinking they're someone else's responsibility to deal with, or that they can't be solved anyway. My hope is that this trip to the dealership will help me explain what's so appealing about a colossal car.

We walk out to the lot of shining metal, and I tell Robert how I used to feel safe in my Jeep Cherokee, but how even that started to feel small with all those other SUVs on the road.

"Well, take your pick," he says, extending his arm toward the rows of Hummers, and I point to the school bus yellow one.

He says, "I'll go get the tags," and disappears into the showroom, leaving me beside the sculpted steel and chrome, the chrome that the brochure claims is included to "elevate the aesthetic." The "elevated aesthetic" reminds me more of a skyscraper or a bulldozer than a car, an actual car that I could drive on actual roads, next to motorcycles and bike riders and schoolchildren. I can't stop thinking that this car is for people who've stopped caring. I also can't quiet that little voice reminding me that I'm not in a great position to throw stones, what with only recently having moved out of my glass house.

I open the Hummer's door and attempt to step gracefully into the driver's seat, but I end up grappling and swinging from the car as though I were a tiny monkey. I feel even tinier inside, dwarfed by the size of the cushy leather seats and the moonroof that spans forever like the horizon in the desert, conveniences of the more suburban, less militaristic second-generation Hummers, the H2s and H3s. I rest my hand on the chrome, utilitarian gearshift and fiddle with the swanky stereo system, satellite radio with no commercials. This truck is a strange blend of machismo and regal indulgence—like if a tank accidentally drove onto the set of *Masterpiece Theatre*, and decided to stay.

Robert shows me the single button that can control all of the windows at superspeed, for busy people who don't like waiting around. There are switches and knobs and levers and buttons everywhere, three just to control the seat position. There's a button to press if you're towing a trailer so that it doesn't push the car or wobble around.

"For towing a boat or a Jet Ski," Robert says.

"I don't have those," I say.

"Maybe you don't have them because you didn't have an easy way to tow them," he says. "And now you do."

The Hummer people seem to have—or envision themselves having—a lot of stuff. They have boats and Ski-Doos. They have CDs to load into the six-CD changer. They have enough electronic gadgets to occupy the car's six power points. They have skis for the roof rack. They have golf clubs to fit in the sprawling trunk. They must also have money to spend on gasoline—with a twenty-five-gallon regular tank and a seventeen-gallon reserve tank, where I'm test-driving in Pennsylvania (this week, with diesel prices at $2.95 per gallon), it would cost me $123.90 every time I went to the gas station. But I have stuff, too—a big dog, a new bureau from IKEA, crap to haul from my basement to the Salvation Army. Could "my Hummer" actually be for me?

AM General started making High Mobility Multipurpose Wheeled Vehicles for the U.S. Army in 1983. The military eventually shortened the acronym HMMWV to the not-exactly-phonetic Humvee (maybe because Humwiv doesn't have the same ring to it). In 1992, AM General introduced a civilian version of the HMMWV to sell to the public, the first time the car was officially called a Hummer; at that point, General Motors owned Hummer. AM General sold them the rights to the name in 1999 but still produced the H2 (the H3 was assembled in GM factories and the H1 was discontinued in 2006). Hummer came out with the H3 in 2006. It seemed like a smaller, more reasonable Hummer, one that promised to be better on gas mileage and more maneuverable in heavy traffic. Hummer Lite, if you will. When I first saw a magazine ad for the H3, I remember feeling proud of Americans, about what a benevolent power we were to demand that our cars—and our lifestyles in general—stop endlessly supersizing at a cost to our wallets and our environment and our safety. The photograph of the scaled-down H3 made me believe in the sincere goodness of American ingenuity the same way my great-grandparents must have felt upon seeing the first images of the Model T. That's when I noticed the capital letters off to the left of the page, just beneath the word *Hummer:* EVEN WHEN WE GO SMALL, WE GO BIG.

In April 2009, GM went bankrupt. Hummer was all set to ditch America and be sold to a Chinese company, Sichuan Tengzhong Heavy Industrial Machinery Company, for around $500 million; the deal fell through, and Hummer production ceased in 2010.

Though Hummers are bigger, they sit on the same frame as GM's other trucks and sport utility vehicles, such as the Suburban, Tahoe, Yukon, and Escalade. Bigger than a Tahoe, named after the lake that contains 39 trillion gallons of water. Bigger than a Yukon, a 483,450-square-kilometer region of Canada. If cars are trees, the Hummer is a sequoia. If cars are buildings, the Hummer is Trump Tower. And if cars are countries, the Hummer is America.

Hummers are classified by the government as Class 3 trucks, but they do not require a special license to drive. The difference between the Suburban and myriad other SUVs, which are now mostly made for city and highway driving, and the Hummer is that the Hummer is still designed to be used off-road. This is a car that can climb a sixteen-inch vertical roadblock. It can drive over a 60 percent grade, a 40 percent side slope, and through thirty inches—that's two and a half feet—of water. This is a car to make us feel prepared for tsunamis or Osama bin Laden, to appease all fear of what we cannot control. In these cars, we are big and rich and menacing and no one would dare mess with us. *Salon* called Hummers a "celebrated and reviled as a metaphor for American bravado—and wretched American excess," as well as a "military-porn embodiment of America's post-9/11 belligerence." In these cars, we can drive over mountains, through rivers.

"Start her up," Robert says, giving directions out of the parking lot and onto the highway. But, oh. Even though I'm used to driving my SUV, my dad's big SUV, and my brother's bigger SUV, I can't stop thinking, *Oh, no no*. I'm panicking. I can't do this. You actually expect me to drive this thing? Don't I need some kind of special license? An operating manual? And what if I kill someone?

I stop and wait to turn right out of the dealership. When I press on the gas, used to the quick pickup of my Jeep, nothing happens. I press harder, and we zoom onto the highway. The car drives as smooth as pudding. We stop at a light behind a station wagon, a car that used to be considered big, and it feels like we're double its height and its width.

"This car feels as big as a tank," I say.

"It is safe, but it's really not that big," Robert says. "See that station wagon ahead of us? You're not any bigger than that, it's just you're squared off, so it seems bigger."

Since a Hummer is more than two feet higher than a Honda Accord, and weighs twice as much, Hummer buyers are quite obviously looking for a sense of physical superiority. So why do the salesman and all the glossy brochures keep insisting it's *not that big*? Are they just telling us what we want to hear, assuaging our guilt, singing us a lullaby, passing us the Kool-Aid we're so thirsty for?

There was a spike in Hummer sales after 9/11, when customers were forced to wait for months to take home a Hummer, even bidding above the sticker price in an attempt to get one. In a *New York Times* article, "Detroit's Hottest Item Is Its Biggest Gas Guzzler," dealers said they could keep only a six-day supply of Hummers on their lots—they were "selling as many of these vehicles as they can get." Not only were Hummers flying off the lots, but they were also the only Big Three brand "selling largely without any national incentives." In just a three-month span in 2002, 7,500 H2s were sold, the most to people in Los Angeles, Miami, and Texas.

A reporter from the BBC wrote that after 9/11, the most "striking and immediate impact on buying patterns has been the rush to improve individual security." And a huge military-inspired car can certainly feel like it improves individual security. Cultural critics have pointed to the endless cycle of fear and consumption, especially how, post-9/11, many of us felt a heightened state of anxiety. We knew we couldn't control whether our plane was the one crashing into New York, or whether our office was on the seventy-sixth floor, or whether our drinking water was swimming with smallpox. We were freaked out. So maybe that's why more Americans were willing to do the one thing we could control: buy a Hummer as big and tough as a military tank, one that can drive up mountains, through rivers of blood, over pyres of burning rubble.

In 2002, *The New York Times* reported that GM dealers had built new showrooms to resemble military barracks, with plenty of brushed steel and exposed bolts. Bergstrom Hummer, in Milwaukee, even erected a thirty-five-foot-high *H* in front of the dealership. But the Hummer is obviously not the first big car in America. Both the road trip and the big car are quintessentially American, storied and mythologized in the American past. In May 2001, when Ari Fleischer was President Bush's press secretary, Fleischer was asked about whether Americans should consider changing our lifestyle to consume less energy, considering we consume more energy per capita than any country in the world. Fleischer responded with an emphatic "No." He went on to say, "The president believes that it's an American way of life, and that it should be the goal of policy makers to protect the American way of life. The American way of life is a blessed one."

And he's right. Embarrassingly, it's how the American way is viewed by much of the rest of the world—not giving two shits about gas prices, or the ozone, or what happens when you crash your three-ton car into someone else. *Sucks to be all of you!* driving a Hummer screams. *But it's great to be me!*

The New York Times reported that starting in 2002, after some handy tax code finagling by the Bush administration, a Hummer owner could deduct $34,912 of the $48,800 base price.

In 2000, Toyota introduced Americans to the Great Green Hope: the forty-plus-miles-per-gallon gas-electric hybrid Prius. It was priced at $20,000—cheaper than an SUV, but accessible mostly to the ecoconscious upper middle class and up, dubbed "Prius Progressives." Celebrities piled on board, lauding the green machines: Leonardo DiCaprio showed up to a big flashy movie premiere in one; Larry David (his then-wife an environment activist) drove one on *Curb Your Enthusiasm*. *The Washington Post* called the cars "Hollywood's latest politically correct status symbol." Though the Prius is sold in forty countries, nearly 60 percent of all sales are in North America, with most of the rest selling in Japan. A few private companies, like Google and Bank of America, offered its employees several thousand dollars in reimbursements for buying a Prius. Some state governments offered tax credits; some counties in California even exempt Priuses from having to pay at parking meters. In its first seven years, Toyota reported selling more than half a million of the hybrids, making it seem, for at least a moment, that green (if not *small*) might replace big. As a point of comparison, the H2 uses more energy for its manufacture and first 24,000 miles of fuel than the Prius does over its entire lifetime.

The first version of the Prius was marketed between the Echo and the Corolla in the Toyota fleet. But Americans wanted a *bigger* greenmobile. Toyota listened, redesigning it to be six inches longer than the early version. The Prius now occupies a different spot in the Toyota size hierarchy, between the Corolla and the Camry.

The next Great Green Hope in the pipeline is the Chevy Volt, due out in 2010. It's an electric car that people have been excitedly talking about since GM killed its electric car a decade ago. Charge the Volt's lithium-ion battery and the car will go forty miles without using *any* gas. Still, it's hard to tell whether mainstream Americans will ever go for it, or if ecocars will always be the realm of Hollywood and the wealthy, guilty-conscience elite.

"What about gas mileage?" I say.

"It's actually pretty good on gas, about seventeen miles per gallon," says Robert.

GM doesn't report the gas mileage for Hummers, but actual users say they tend to get about ten to twelve miles per gallon. And since Hummers each have a gross vehicle weight rating of above

8,500 pounds, they fall under the classification of "heavy vehicles," similar to shuttle buses and ambulances; as such, the EPA does not release their gas mileage ratings. Also, because they're considered Class 3 trucks, Hummers are exempt from many Department of Transportation safety regulations, such as passive restraints and third brake lights. And under President Bush's tax plan, some business owners could legally deduct up to $100,000 for their Hummer purchases, because the vehicle weighs more than 6,000 pounds. You can find other aggravating Hummer facts on the Web site for the group Fuck You and Your H2 (www.fuh2.com), which also publishes thousands of photos of people flipping off H2s.

Well, what about these pissed-off, anti-Hummer activists? Are they, as some Hummer owners argue (invoking a line much-used by overweight strippers on the *Jerry Springer* show), just jealous? With a good amount of conviction, I can say I doubt that. The anti-Hummer people were my old crew. Young and politically active, militant live-small vegans—we were people living for the cause. When I was one of them, I felt superior for *not* having a Hummer, the same way I assumed Hummer owners must feel superior *for* having one; I just figured that both groups had an equal level of pride in their ownership or nonownership. We wouldn't get in your Hummer, even if you offered us a ride to the G8 protest.

Sometimes driving my Jeep around a few years later, I'd think of my old friends. Some of them—the ones whom I saw only when running into them by chance, who could, without a word, make me feel embarrassed about my decisions—were still getting tattoos on their necks, still piling in a van and driving to D.C. to march. Some of us went the Pottery Barn route, and these are the friends from that group whom I am still close with—likely because we made similar decisions, to get mortgages and eat meat and buy stuff that wasn't from a thrift store and to drive around in big cars. We helped one another forget where we came from and not feel as ashamed of where we were going.

The Earth Liberation Front is perhaps the most extreme example of pissed-off vigilantes, people I would've known through mutual friends, but never been close to. The group caused $1 million worth of damage in the end of 2003 by setting fire to Hummers at a California dealership. They also claimed responsibility for spray-painting slogans such as "Fat, Lazy Americans" on SUVs at other dealerships in the state. They don't just want to boycott Hummers themselves; they don't want you driving yours, either.

It's apparent that lots of non-Hummer owners love feeling superior. Even though I had an SUV—so in many people's minds I was just as guilty—I still loved to point fingers at the Hummer owners. It's a tiny bit of the satisfaction I felt as a live-small devotee, then free to wash my hands of the war in Iraq, the blood spilled for oil, the drilling in Alaska's Arctic National Wildlife Refuge. I loved the feeling of eschewing all responsibility, placing the blame entirely on others who increased the oil demand. It's an appealing moral liberty, and my old anarchy-kid-on-a-bike self wasn't the only one clinging to it. Many hybrid car owners, MINI Cooper owners, even smaller-SUV owners like myself could agree on one thing: blame the Hummer people.

But I know I'm implicated, too. More than once I stopped at a red light next to a Hummer and looked out my window and thought, *Why do they need that abomination? They're never going to take it off-*

road, and they're using too much gasoline, and they only want that car because they think it looks cool, and why aren't they riding the bus, anyway? I thought this, though, while looking at a Hummer through the window of my Jeep, which I only took off-road once in the three years I owned it, and which used more gasoline than I really needed, I wasn't riding the bus, either. Damn. So if most of us are also contributing to the SUV problems of pollution and traffic and war for oil, then why do we allow ourselves such contempt for the Hummer people? Aren't they doing what we're doing, only they're doing it bigger and better? Are we displacing anger with our own responsibility, compounded by our own guilt, and projecting it onto them, an easy-to-identify enemy? Is it just easier to hate the Hummer than to hate ourselves?

I decided to talk with some Hummer people in hopes of better seeing their side of the story. Hal Dilworth and his wife, Georgia, have owned three Hummers. The two are middle-aged Floridians who seem kind, hardworking, and down-to-earth. Hal is a finance manager at a Cadillac dealership, but he wasn't exactly on board when his dealership first started selling Hummers in 2003.

"I thought they were pretty dumb. [Georgia and I] had always been car people," Hal says. "I thought, *Why did anybody* need *anything like that?* Not because of gas or anything—it was more that the pure size of the vehicle seemed completely unnecessary." But then the dealership started running events, off-roading on a sprawling nearby ranch, which forced him to get behind the wheel. "I just fell in love. I loved off-roading in the mountains, the people I met, the kind of spirit of it." Though he's driven his share of cars and trucks, Hal says he was "amazed by the pure unbelievable operative capability of the vehicle." That said, "If you would have told us five years ago that we would be driving around in the woods in a Hummer, climbing over rocks, driving up and down mountains, we would have told you you're crazy."

Hal describes Hummer people as "from all walks of life," but narrows that down, saying they "tend to have fairly conservative political viewpoints" and be financially "upper middle class, since this is an expensive toy." When I ask him about people who hate on Hummer owners, he shrugs it off. "There are misconceptions and stereotypes about Hummer owners just like there are about blondes or car salesmen," he says. "Whatever. You get over it." He tells me he's never gotten any attitude, but then corrects himself, remembering one time at a gas station when a guy told him he was "a stupid ass for having a Hummer," so he just flipped the guy off on his way out. Though Hal insists that his off-roading crew doesn't look down on Hummer owners who never get off the suburban pavement, he does tell me the name for them: Street Queens.

Though the Dilworths have a smaller H3 now, Hal's wife, Georgia, preferred when they had the larger, more militaristic H1. Georgia also goes off-roading, but she primarily used the H1 for getting to and from work every day. "Sometimes people would salute her when she drove by, maybe thinking it was a military vehicle," Hal says.

"I've never gotten flipped off or any negative looks," says Georgia. "But have I gotten *looks*? Oh, yeah—as a woman driving one, guys are always looking at you."

Driving a Hummer is a confidence-booster for Georgia in other ways too. "When you go off-road, you say to yourself, 'Did I really just drive this vehicle through that huge pile of rocks, or this big ol' lake of water? Yeah, I did!'"

The couple bonds over Hummers, with Hal calling Georgia from his cell phone to report on the H1 that he's behind on the expressway.

With Hal's job at a dealership, they have access to myriad makes and models, but Georgia still assures me, "There will be a Hummer in our future for a long time."

The way we anthropomorphize the Hummer—overblown, macho, physically massive, not to be messed with—sounds a lot like how we think of Arnold Schwarzenegger. So it's no surprise that he's made himself the unofficial face of the Hummer, ready to crush any girly-man car. Schwarzenegger was instrumental in convincing AM General to produce the civilian-use Hummer, so it's not much of a surprise that in 1992, he became the first civilian to own one. Since then, at various points he's owned seven of them, earning him the nickname Governor Hummer.

Schwarzenegger subsequently rushed to go ecofriendly and instead nab the nickname of the Green Governor. He got GM to develop one hydrogen-powered Hummer, with a million-dollar-plus price tag, and another converted from diesel to biofuel. He sold a few of his Hummers—he was usually being driven by the California Highway Patrol anyhow—and kept the rest in storage. In 2006, he told the *San Francisco Chronicle*, "As far as my Hummers are concerned, they are very safely stored in some warehouse garage. I have not had an opportunity to drive them, but I don't think they are polluting the air or ocean sitting in the garage." If he knew that huge Hummers were so stigmatized in this suddenly green environment—especially in California—why not just make a statement by getting rid of them? "Protecting the environment does not require us to be against large SUVs or trucks," he told *Spiegel* in 2007. "Instead, we should develop technology to cut down greenhouse gas emissions . . . it's not about what the size of the car is . . . that doesn't mean that you should take this big car and make it smaller. Instead, we should be saying: 'Keep the luxury car!' "

I'm not a very technical Hummer driver, with questions about horsepower or cylinders or catalytic converters. I picked my particular Jeep because it was what the dealership called "flame" red (and my friend called "seduction, seduction" red, and the local police called "No, you're not getting off with just a warning" red).

So it was strange when, several years ago, I noticed a car enough to comment on it. I was in France, where my attention was drawn less to the cars than the women in flouncy skirts and stilettos, zipping around on their bicycles and Vespas. I admired the narrow, cobblestone streets. I noticed all of this as I walked home from drinking along the Seine with some other American, non-car-noticing women. We were lamenting that all of the best patisseries in Saint-Germain-des-Prés were closed at this hour, and as we crossed the street, we saw it: the Smart car. It was so tiny that I half expected a boy with a remote control to be following behind. It was abrupt and silly, like if a regular sedan accidentally parked under a guillotine, and the back got chopped off. My friends and I laughed. We laughed so hard—this was an actual car? In the actual street?—that we clung to one another to remain standing. Later in the week, we found a parked Smart car and took more pictures of ourselves in front of it than the Eiffel Tower. It seemed one of those quintessentially European things, something that would never, could never, cross over to America, the land of the urban tank, the home of the Hummer.

Nonetheless, in 2008, Smart cars finally arrived on this side of the pond. But I mostly saw negative write-ups and laments about its actual gas mileage, which is less than that of a Prius. A *New York Times* reviewer summed up the Smart car: "With its limited carrying capacity, seemingly mediocre fuel economy, erratic handling and fitful acceleration, one question that potential buyers in this part of the world should be asking is, what's the point?" Ouch.

So I decided to test-drive a car that might be more practical for me: a MINI Cooper. I picked out one that was the same color red as my Jeep. As soon as I got out of the parking lot, I stepped on the gas, zooming and stopping and weaving in a way that made me turn up the radio and think, *Awwww, yeah!* I pressed the button to open the panoramic moonroof. I felt like I was in complete control, like when I still had training wheels on my bike but knew I didn't need them anymore, but kept them on for a few extra weeks so I could be fast and reckless and zip around corners without wobbling. I pulled into a lot to try parking, choosing a spot that in my Jeep would've required some delicate backing up and inching forward and turning maneuvers. I handled it effortlessly. I thought: *why hasn't all of America jumped on the tiny-car bandwagon? Can't we organize some kind of massive test-drive?* I thought, *Why did I ever own an SUV?* I thought, *Will this make my old friends think I'm less of a sellout?*

I came to a stoplight. I was singing along to Mick Jagger on the radio, belting out, "You can't always get what you want." I felt good. I felt like I could buy this car, could save myself and my country and the environment, all at once. And then I turned to look out my window, singing the "You get what you neeeeeed" part to the pedestrians on the corner. Except, there were no pedestrians.

There was not even a road. In its place was a tank. Only not a tank but a Hummer, or the wheel of a Hummer, filling up my field of vision as if a picture of the world's biggest tire with the world's shiniest rims had been painted onto my window. I thought about what would happen if that car accidentally slid into this one. I imagined that giant, shiny tire crushing through my cockpitlike dashboard, and over my dog yelping in the backseat, and over my bags of groceries, tomatoes and jugs of milk exploding under the weight.

In a second I understood why people might not be jumping on the tiny-car bandwagon. My favorite part of the song still hummed in the background, but I drove to the dealership in silence, handed over the keys, and went home.

I'm back in my Hummer remembering this wheel-filling-up-my-window moment, which makes me start to wonder about the spectrum, about how similar most of us really are to these Hummer people. They make me angry, both with them and with myself. I think about how terrible Hummers are for the environment, how I should've traded in my Jeep for a MINI Cooper, and then traded my MINI Cooper in for a bicycle, to live with less impact even if it meant less convenience. Logically, I knew I didn't need a giant SUV, and I know that not many other people do, either. But then I think about how the Hummer people and Escalade people and Tahoe people and millions of other people who are all driving huge trucks, trucks that could crush me without even noticing, and I think, *Forget the environment.* Forget the war for oil in Iraq. Forget everyone's else's safety. If people are going to drive gigantic cars and cause gigantic threats to the environment—and to me if I get in a collision with them—then why is it my job to live small?

I'm indulging in this negative chain of thought when Robert snaps me out of it by telling me that buying a Hummer will actually help protect the environment. Huh? "You'll also be part of a community," he says, handing me a glossy brochure. He then explains about the Hummer Driving Academy, in which I can learn to drive my Hummer in "ditch crossings, water crossings, and boulder navigation." As part of the franchise agreement, each Hummer dealership is required to host a minimum of four off-road driving events every year.

"They also have Hummers you can rent once you get there, so you don't get yours all muddy," he says.

After the driving academy part of the brochure, which discusses all the wildlife my hulking car and I can run over, is a section called Tread Lightly! that explains how Hummer owners have a responsibility to "protect terrain and its fragile ecosystems." Which is why, as a Hummer owner, you also receive a free lifetime membership to Tread Lightly!, a nonprofit group that protects land and water resources.

"It's cool, if you're into that kind of thing," Robert says.

Lots of people are, in fact, into that kind of thing, and all kinds of other Hummer-themed programs. The national Hummer Club is a nonprofit that boasts six hundred dues-paying members; they even have a quarterly magazine. Hal Dilworth is a board member of the Hummer Club. He tells me that they're "a very welcoming group of people, no matter if you have an H1, an H2, or an H3. No matter what you do for a living, whether you're male or female, young or old, black or white. We embrace people because they have a Hummer." Mostly, they run daylong or weekendlong off-road events, testing themselves and showing newcomers how to navigate their big shiny trucks over rocks, through streams, between trees. They also do local events, like Hummer Night at the Quaker Steak & Lube restaurant, "where everybody shines their truck up and then shows them off in the parking lot," says Hal.

If it's easy to roll your eyes at a Hummer, it's even more tempting to do so with the Hummer Club. But Hal tells me that many members are also part of the HOPE program (Hummer Owners Prepared for Emergencies), a partnership between the American Red Cross and the Hummer Club. That means the Hummer owners are trained in off-road driving by the Hummer Club and certified in CPR and first aid techniques by the Red Cross. In case of hurricanes, floods, tornados, or other disasters, HOPE members use their Hummers to deliver supplies like food, water, and medication, or to pick people up to see doctors who couldn't get out for medical attention otherwise, due to something like high water; I can't help but think of the HOPE drivers as brethren to the civilian boat owners who rescued people during Hurricane Katrina.

"We just make ourselves and our resources and our trucks available to help the community," Hal says. Every Christmas, lots of club members also load up their trucks with supplies for the Toys for Tots program.

"How can you flip off a guy who's taking toys to kids who don't have toys?" Hal says.

Though they don't have local chapters, the club runs about fifteen events every year in different parts of the country, usually in California, Washington, Utah, Tennessee, Michigan, and Alabama; they don't do many in Florida, the Dilworths' home state, "because we don't have any hills," says Georgia. The group is made up of "people from all walks of life who share a common interest, and no matter what you do or where you come from or what your background is, you're drawn together purely by the vehicle," Hal explains, going on to compare the Hummer Club as similar to the way people "might be drawn together in a church, but you're drawn together by the allure of a vehicle."

And I believe him. There's some special draw to Hummers. Before they bought their first Hummer, Georgia drove a tiny two-seater sports car. She and Hal went to a club event for that model, but they didn't get hooked. "We got there and these people were dressed to match their cars. We were like, 'Oh, man, this is weird.' We never went back," Hal says. "I can't say exactly what it was, but the Hummer Club was different."

Now they're hooked. "Promoting the [Hummer] lifestyle is critical to the survival of the brand and the Club as we know it today," he says.

Robert suggests I upgrade my Hummer package to include a chrome brush guard in front of the car's grille. This costs an extra $525, but he doesn't mention that.

"It'll protect your car," he says.

More likely than rogue branches, I'd need the brush guard to protect my lights from breaking when I accidentally roll this titanic car into a telephone pole.

Except that when he asks me to turn into a parking lot and pull this massive rectangle of steel into a space made for normal cars, I can do it. I think I must be crooked, or taking up three spots, or pinning several stray shoppers beneath my massive tires, but when I get out to look, I've done it perfectly.

"Perfect!" Robert says, over and over. "You're a natural."

I can't believe that me, five-foot-three-in-high-heels me, always got hit in the head by a ball in gym class me, is driving this massive, hulking beast, and doing it well. My ego swells. I get back into the car, this time feeling more like a rock star and less like a monkey.

Robert warns me the Hummer is not an amphibious vehicle, nor a submarine. It cannot float. He does not advise driving it in tsunamis or blizzards. Military Humvees do have a snorkel kit extending the exhaust and air intake to roof level, making it possible to operate in sixty inches of water (just about how tall I stand). I have to pause to take in the James Bond factor of the U.S. military driving snorkeling cars. I know that in a million years, I would never use this feature—if there's five feet of water, I should probably either drive around it or go home—but for a moment, I want to know I have it. But the civilian Hummers cannot use the snorkel kit because certain parts aren't waterproof. I understand why the military needs such big, bad trucks—but why do soccer moms?

What is it about civilian-use Hummers that seems so American? Is it simply because they're big? Because they're self-important, or awe-inspiring, or ostentatious? And what is so quintessentially American about having more car than you could ever possibly need?

In 2007, Hummer sales dropped 22 percent; by 2008, they were down 50 percent. That same year, gas prices continually ticked upward, climbing month by month. By July of 2008, gas jumped to an all-time high price of $4.12 for a gallon of regular, basically threatening to kill the road trip, the SUV, and the summer vacation in one fell swoop. A few months later, stocks plummeted, and millions of Americans watched their retirement accounts go worthless overnight. To make matters worse, the Big Three American automakers also went broke and cut jobs. Some begged the U.S. government for a $15 billion in bailout loans to save these giants of Detroit, like Chrysler and General Motors, who made the Hummer.

Would these dire circumstances turn Hummers and other gas-guzzlers from ubiquitous suburban vehicles into dinosaurs of the road, relics of a bygone era?

Well, no. Just five months after the country reported its highest gas prices, we saw some relief. By December 2008, the national average for a gallon of regular had dropped to $1.75, the lowest price since March 2004.

Americans breathed a collective sigh of relief . . . and then went back to business as usual.

In fact, by March 2009 (with gas prices down to about half of peak prices), dealers had changed their tunes. Instead of gas-guzzlers languishing on the lots and hybrids flying off the same day they arrived, gas-guzzlers were moving (okay, not flying—*no* cars were) and hybrids were the ones languishing. In a *Wall Street Journal* article entitled "Industry's Big Hope for Small Cars Fades," car dealers reported half a million gas-sippers piled up on lots around the country. As a general auto dealer rule, a healthy supply of cars in stock is fifty to sixty days' worth. In July, when gas prices topped out, dealers could only keep about a nine-day supply of the subcompact Honda Fit. By March, though, they were stuck with 125 days' worth.

Why wasn't the gas hike a reflective, even instructive moment? Why didn't we realize that maybe gas prices would eventually skyrocket again, and that this might be a good time to rethink the size of the standard American automobile? Why didn't the several-month stretch of "big is bad" leave any kind of lasting tarnish? Beau Boeckmann has an idea. He's vice president of Galpin Motors

Inc., the highest sales volume Ford dealer in the world, and a con-sulting producer for MTV's *Pimp My Ride*. In a blog post, he noted that when gas prices shot up and Americans immediately dashed out for small cars, "It was a reaction to gas prices, not, say: 'I don't need a truck. It's the right thing for the environment if I buy a smaller car.' Americans are very reactive in their deci-sions . . . it wasn't a permanent change of attitude." Which is ex-actly why when gas prices dropped, so did our fervor for minisized cars.

He told *The Wall Street Journal*, "I don't think Americans really like small cars. They drive them when they think they have to, when gas prices are high." Exactly right.

But Boeckmann's argument about why we prefer big doesn't seem less convincing, that notion that "we're big people and we like big cars." He says Americans buy trucks and large SUVs "based on a need, not because it is the cool thing to be seen in." It's because lots of Americans are both tall and wide, making smaller cars less fea-sible. It's true that being the fattest country in the world probably means we need our cars to be supersized, too, which explains why some heavy people would drive bigger cars. And that could ex-plain why physically hulking celebrities—LeBron James, Mike Tyson, Dennis Rodman, David Beckham, 50 Cent—all own Hummers.

But are we really supposed to believe there's not a cool factor, that our biggest stars are only choosing their cars out of necessity? Lots of people buy Hummers because they think the cars are cool and flashy; the most expensive packages set the cost of a new H2 at about $120,000. Tupac Shakur rapped about having one. Hugh Hef-ner has one. Oscar-winning movie stars, like Adrien Brody, have Hummers. They're rich; they're famous; they're not Mike Tyson—

sized. Lots of Americans want to be like them, if not *be* them, and driving their same car is just a more expensive—and decidedly, more male—version of the Jennifer Aniston haircut craze. (Paris Hilton drives one, incidentally.) So many Americans, especially celebrities, wouldn't seek out big cars if there weren't big status or big power attached. And we indoctrinate early; the children's toy company Nikko sells a perfect-to-scale, remote control H2 for $99.99.

Robert wants to think of some vanity plates for me. On the full fold-out poster of an H2 that he's included with my brochures, he writes in capitals letters: "Y NOT" and "GRRL TOY," the page flapping over the center console.

"I'm going to make this even nicer for you," Robert says. He flips a switch to turn on the heated seat, and it feels so lush and fabulous that I realize I will never again sit in a chair this comfortable, outside of Brookstone. Then he flips down a little leather novelty armrest, and I'm struck by the adorableness of such a tiny detail in such a looming, enormous car. For a moment, a telegraphic message from the past flashes through my conscience: *There! Are! People! Starving!*, but I just set my elbow on the armrest and keep driving. It is soft and cushy and warm, and this radio station is playing my favorite song with no commercials.

"I have the perfect plate for you," Robert says, and then pauses for a moment.

"H2 BAR B," he says, enunciating each letter. "Get it? Like Barbie?"

Oh, I get it. I laugh and accelerate up the hill, feel the power under the hood like a volcano waiting to go off as soon as I say go. I'm feeling tough and powerful and luscious and sexy. We fly past

the other cars, filled with tiny, boring people. I'm a huge, shiny
monster; I can crush you without breaking a nail. Get the hell out
of my way. I'm driving this H2, and it's yellow like nylon Barbie
hair and its tires are four feet high and the engine zooms like a bus
on PCP and I could squash your little Hondas like toys, and did I
mention you should get the hell out of my way? I am rich and tough
and I have this real-life Tonka truck and I could run over you and
your car and your mom's car all stacked on top of each other and not
even feel it, because my seats are leather and heated and comfortable
like I should be sitting by a fire, reading Shakespeare, but I could
drive sideways up Mount Everest and laugh at the people with their
rappelling gear—people, human people, walking, actually walking, when they could be in this car, this huge and giant and fabulous
car that makes me a rock star, only much tougher, like a professional
prize-fighter rock star, except more glamorous, like a professional
prize-fighter rock star with velvet elbow-length gloves and a ciga-
rette holder.

Clearly, those new-car-smell chemicals have gone to my head.

"This car might intimidate some guys," Robert warns me. "But
only the weak ones, the kind you wouldn't want anyway."

I imagine the litany of my former boyfriends: skinny, cardigan-
wearing, bespectacled vegans. Then I imagine the kind of man who
would look good sitting next to me in this car: tanned from Saint-
Tropez, wine-drinking, with muscles thick like truck tires pushing
up against his shirt with the little alligator logo. Our voices ringing
out in unison, we'll shout, "Get the hell out of our way!"

"It definitely sends a message. You know, not *everyone* can drive
a Hummer."

"I know," I say. "Oh, I know." I hear the words come out in a voice I don't recognize as my own. They resonate with entitlement, bouncing off the leather and glass and chrome, and settle on my skin with the delicate sting of pinpricks. I cringe. I hear the voice-over from the 1980s public service announcement: "This is your brain. This is your brain on Hummer."

I know now that I wouldn't allow myself to buy a Hummer—my inner hippie, though dormant, still exists. But I also see the glamour and the allure of shushing that inner voice by running it the hell over, squashing all your guilt with that temporary rush, the ecstasy of being free to do and have whatever you want.

"I think it's time to turn around," I say.

"Just remind me to take a picture," Robert says, "for your fridge."

8.
MALL OF AMERICA

One thing's for sure: if you can't find what you're
looking for here, America doesn't have it.

—MALL OF AMERICA SECTION OF TWIN CITIES GUEST GUIDE

At the Mall of America, you can buy: curry-flavored peanut butter. Or white
chocolate raspberry-flavored peanut butter. Or sun-dried tomato–flavored
peanut butter. Or one of twelve other peanut butters for sale at P.B. Loco.

The wall of noise inside the Mall of America is: Making. Me.
Nuts. I've been here for twenty-four hours. They wouldn't let
me do twenty-four hours straight (the MOA isn't open for that
long, but more than that, its managers probably realized it would be
some kind of cruel psychological endurance test). So I've been
here—walking, sitting, running my hands over racks of clothes,
shuffling behind slow walkers, and taking pit stops to eat—for eight
hours. Eight hours a day for three days in a row. At this point, it's
the noise that's nearly driving me out of the mall, shrieking into the
parking lot. Though the top floor has bland indoor-outdoor carpeting, the other floors are brown square tiles. Follow the brown
brick road and you'll spend the next several years of your life looping around and around the same floor. After awhile, maybe hour
five, it starts to feel like being on a treadmill—you can feel you're
moving, but the scenery never changes. This mall, in Bloomington,
Minnesota, in the suburbs of Minneapolis, disorients with its over-
stimulation. It could be any mall in any American suburb; it could

be day or night; it could be hot or snowy. When I'm inside, there's no way to know—and I get the feeling that's how they like it. A *New York Times* article aptly called the MOA "the mother of all malls, a pioneer in the field of destination retailing, and a sprawling, visceral economic indicator."

After eight hours inside the mall, the noise is like being inside a blender. You hear feet shuffling, kids' sneakers screeching to a stop, babies crying, the bleating of goats from the petting zoo, cell phones chiming, children asking their parents for toys. This is what I imagine it must be like for a baby: you hear so many different noises at once, loud and indiscriminant, that none stands out and they blend together into an aural Monet—a vague impression of the mall, with no sharp edges. There's no music in the endless hallways, but each store's playing its own soundtrack themed up to what kind of demographic would shop there, and the instant juxtaposition of Avril Lavigne and Frank Sinatra is a mix tape that should never exist.

"The shopping mall is thought of as an American invention, and America as the mall capital of the world," says Paco Underhill, author of *Call of the Mall*. James J. Farrell, the author of *One Nation Under Goods: Malls and the Seductions of American Shopping*, echoes that, saying, "Though American malls have been around for less than a century, their influence on our culture has been amazing." Today, the average American makes thirty-eight trips to a mall every year. The first American shopping center opened in the 1920s in Kansas City, Missouri, but the first American mall that bears resemblance to what we think of as malls today was the 1950s-era Southdale Center, which was built in Minnesota (like the Mall of America). That prototype of the Southdale Center "set the standard for a whole generation of shopping centers—enclosed, fully air-conditioned, anchored by department stores, with lots of public and pedestrian spaces, surrounded by parking lots, all under one management. That model, now replicated all over the world, helped Americans (and imitators worldwide) increase per capita consumption astronomically in the late twentieth century," says Farrell. He points out that malls "serve as cultural indicators of American assumptions about need and sufficiency, status and class, race and gender. They are a showcase for how Americans work and play." We go to the mall a lot—a study by the International Council of Shopping Centers shows that men and women both hit the mall more than nine times in a three-month period.

There are so many choices here, so many more than in a regular mall. I've been walking for miles. My head's filled with white noise. I keep thinking about a story my friend told me about when she first came home to Boston from her assignment in the Peace Corps in Burkina Faso and how a trip to the shampoo aisle of a grocery store made her have a nervous breakdown.

For a moment, after roughly the twenty-hour mark at the Mall of America, I can begin to understand how she felt.

At the Mall of America, you can buy: a Garrison Keillor sweatshirt and matching mug from Lake Wobegon, U.S.A., a store based on Keillor's radio show, *A Prairie Home Companion.* Most of the shirts are green.

The mall is a spectacle, a national monument to consumerism. It has 520 stores, an indoor amusement park with roller coasters, a petting zoo. The Mall of America is one of the most visited attractions in America. Forty percent of its visitors are tourists. Every year, more people visit the Mall of America than Disney World, Graceland, and the Grand Canyon combined.

I see my reflection in the Mall of America's endless miles of store windows. I think about how this mall is the pinnacle of temptation—always another store, always something else to want. I can see why so many people who come here succumb to that hungry wanting feeling, a little voice that repeats, "Buy more."

If it feels, as you walk through the Mall of America, as though you've been walking forever, that's because it is, by square footage, the largest mall in the United States. It has a total floor area of 4.2 million square feet, spread over four levels. According to the Shopping Mall and Shopping Center Studies department at Eastern Connecticut State University, "Large malls actively promote their size with pride, implying that they offer a greater variety of merchandise or a richer consumer experience in comparison with their smaller competitors." The average person spends $129 per visit to the MOA, while shoppers at other malls around the country spend an average of $83.30. What is it about a big mall that encourages a person to spend more? The variety, maybe. Studies show that the more stores there are, the more a visitor is likely to spend. Same goes for the longer a person stays at a mall (on average, your total spending goes up $1.01 for every minute you're in the mall), so never-ending structures like the MOA obviously benefit.

Or could it be because in a mall this big, you can never find a limit to the things you want?

At the Mall of America, you can buy: a cold dog, which is like a hot dog, but with ice cream instead of meat and a Twinkie instead of the bun. If they taste a little like goat poop, that's probably because they're sold within smelling distance of the indoor petting zoo.

Paco Underhill has spent his career researching malls, and he thinks the Mall of America is in trouble.

"First of all, it's aged badly. The parking lots are absolutely dismal, with weeds peeking up through the pavement. There's minimal lighting. It's really cold and not particularly inviting," Underhill says. Not to mention the lack of upscale stores.

"The tenant mix, when they opened, tended to be quite high-end. But at this point, they will accept anybody who's willing to pay rent."

So why does it still get so many visitors and make so much money?

"The Mall of America is the only real place to shop between San Francisco and Chicago. People come in from small communities to take a shopping vacation—they spend the weekend here," he says.

It's hardly a surprise that America has a shopping addiction. By the 1980s, the value of thriftiness had become as passé as corduroy bell-bottoms. By the time the '90s hit, no one would be judged for trying to re-create wear-once trendy outfits from *Clueless;* by the 2000s, no one would balk at putting a $28,000 wedding on credit cards and asking bridesmaids to plunk down $300 for a taffeta dress and another $800 for a destination bachelorette party in Vegas. It didn't seem like living large. It seemed, actually, to be living like everyone else.

That may be because we were used to living pretty much like our neighbors. In the 1950s and '60s, the distribution of wealth in America was fairly even. Neal Soss, the chief economist at Credit Suisse, told *The New York Times,* "We had a period of roughly fifty years, from 1929 to 1979, when the income distribution tended to flatten . . . [but] since the early '80s, incomes have tended to get less equal," meaning a fairly reasonable gap between rich and poor turned into a Grand Canyon. By the late 1970s, the superrich had begun pulling away to whole new levels of wealth. For example, in the late 1970s, the cutoff to qualify for the highest-earning bracket for households was roughly $2 million; by 2007, it had jumped to $11.5 million (in inflation-adjusted, pretax terms, as researched by economists Thomas Piketty and Emmanuel Saez). The money stratification hit its peak in the 2000s—by 2006, income was more concentrated at the top than it had been since the late 1920s. But with the recession, the rich stopped getting richer in early 2008, a decades-long reversal of fortune. According to the *Times*, the wealthy elite actually "became poorer . . . and many may not return to their old levels of wealth and income any-time soon."

Welcome to "Affluenza." PBS did a special on the modern con-dition, defining it as "the bloated, sluggish, and unfulfilled feeling that results from efforts to keep up with the Joneses; an epidemic of stress, overwork, waste, and indebtedness caused by dogged pur-suit of the American Dream; an unsustainable addiction to eco-nomic growth."

Dr. April Lane Benson, author of *To Buy or Not to Buy: Why We Overshop and How to Stop* and editor of *I Shop, Therefore I Am: Compulsive Buying and the Search for Self,* blames the "meteoric rise of overshopping" on "the public's radical shift in reference points." Basically, we are still trying to keep up with the Joneses, but who exactly those Joneses are has changed—drastically. Up until thirty years ago, Benson argues, we compared ourselves to the family who lived next door, geographically and economically fairly close to us, or at least within the same stratosphere. But then the mid-'80s hit, bringing us a stock market boom and yuppies and shows like *Lifestyles of the Rich and Famous*, and we started comparing ourselves to the Joneses on TV, who had "a significantly more affluent lifestyle," prompting us to feel like we were worthless unless we got more.

The 2000s took the Joneses to a whole other level. Most often, the people we started seeing on television were the richest of the rich. We got MTV's *My Super Sweet 16*, about fifteen-year-olds whose parents spend a quarter million bucks on their parties, so their children will be the wealthiest, most popular kids in school (who got that way by throwing hissy fits if they didn't get the right color Mercedes SUVs). Bravo became crowded with half a dozen versions of its *Real Housewives* series, about Botoxed, bored-stiff women shopping off their husbands' enormous wealth and living in McMansions (one of the Real Housewives from the Atlanta seasons later foreclosed on hers, not surprisingly off camera). VH1 launched *The Fabulous Life of . . .* revealing what celebrities of the moment spent on houses, cars, vacations, and general upkeep. Oprah was said to fly in her own eyebrow waxer on a private jet; Britney Spears was rumored to have her favorite brand of coffee flown in to her, still hot, wherever she traveled.

When these are the Joneses that we hold ourselves up to, it's no surprise that we never measure up, that we need to keep buying. Overconsuming isn't about keeping up anymore, but rather just staying in the race.

"Shopping itself has become a lifestyle," says Benson.

Shopping makes us happy, at least for a moment. And we want to be happy—hell, the Declaration of Independence gives "the pursuit of happiness" equal weight with liberty and even life itself. We've all heard of "retail therapy," the practice of buying as a pick-me-up. The effects are only temporary, of course, and generally only work for people who are run-of-the-mill blue, not clinically depressed.

Retail therapy seems pretty harmless, especially compared to other, more obviously dangerous ways of decompressing. A 2008 study by researchers at Harvard, Carnegie Mellon, Stanford, and the University of Pittsburgh showed that sad shoppers are willing to pay four times more for the same item than non-sad shoppers. They don't recognize they're shopping to feel better; most of the sad group said their sadness "didn't affect their willingness to spend more." But the study found the opposite to be true: basically, when someone is sad, she feels bad about herself; stuff, especially stuff with a higher price tag, has explicit value, so buying it is a way to show that the *buyer* has value. When we're sad, we're more likely to spend.

I'm as guilty of it as anyone. And shopping is one of the only emotional crutches—compared to, say, overeating, drinking, or drugs—that can make you seem more put together, the owner of a beautifully furnished home or the coolest new gadget or a striking new outfit. Buying things is a comfortable diversion, a cup of coffee at 4:00 P.M. when the day feels like wading through honey. Shopping is something shiny to take your eye away from the ugliness. It's about hope, wishing that what we buy is going to make us prettier or cooler or smarter—and ultimately, happier. Buying is aspirational, not for what we'll possess but for how we'll feel once we have it. In my past shopping trips, when I bought a blazer or button-down shirt, I hoped it would make me feel more confident at work. When I bought my dog a new toy, I hoped it would make me feel less guilty about leaving him alone all day. When I bought a car with leather seats and a CD player, I hoped the traffic-laden commute would be more tolerable. Haven't we all bought something for its promise of making ourselves or our lives better?

But still I had to inch my way in traffic to the office, left my dog alone all day, and felt unprepared to handle a big assignment at work. I still sat awake at night worrying. Most often, at the end of the shopping day, we're left in the same place as before, only with less money and more stuff.

Then there are the serious consequences, both to our bank accounts and our psyches. Compulsive shopping, a condition described as an unstoppable need to buy, is on the rise. A 2006 Stanford School of Medicine study found that 5.8 percent of American adults are overshoppers. Interestingly, it also found that shopping problems affect as many men as women. A 2008 study found that 15 percent of college students showed compulsive buying tendencies. Two major factors in overshopping are people who have "insecurity and chronically low self-esteem" and who have "difficulty tolerating negative moods," says April Lane Benson. They also tend to define happiness as having the most stuff, so they "make acquiring possessions a central goal in life." She quotes psychologist Paul Wachtel: "The more you believe that happiness comes from material wealth, the more likely you are to be depressed, distressed, or anxious." Basically, unhappiness prompts us to spend, and spending does little to fend off our unhappiness. Not long after the receipts are printed, we're broke and dissatisfied.

But don't tell that to the thousands of people milling around me at the Mall of America.

* * *

I talked to Rachel, a twenty-six-year-old Miami woman who admits she's a compulsive shopper. She started binge shopping a few years ago when her marriage was on the rocks.

"I needed to go to the store all the time," she says. "I mean *all* the time. I was spending about $1,200 a month on clothes; I had 150 pairs of shoes, 35 purses, and 25 pairs of sunglasses. But once I bought something, I wasn't really attached to the item; I was attached to going out and getting the next thing. In my two walk-in closets, I had plenty of stuff with the tags still on, but I also gave a lot away because it just doesn't have the same appeal once it's home. I was only using 30 percent of what I owned, but I would still open my closet and say, 'I have nothing to wear.' It wasn't about having or wearing but about acquiring.

"I would go to different branches of the same store because it's uncomfortable when the salespeople recognize you. It's just like being a junkie—you want the fix but you don't want to get caught. I started labeling my friends as ones who would go shopping with me—my partners in crime—and ones who wouldn't. One friend and I would spend fourteen hours at a mall. We called it girls' day out, but that was really our code for going to different malls all day, even driving to malls in other cities.

"My husband and I started keeping separate bank accounts, but I still didn't want him to know what I was spending. So I would hide things, letting bags pile up in the back of my SUV, and then when he was at work, I'd bring all the stuff inside. I would shove things inside my coat or wear them from the car into the house so they didn't seem new. You learn the tricks of disguise.

"Working in a very stressful job as a mortgage account executive, shopping was my way of treating myself. I may have had a deadline, but I'd be on eBay or www.ninewest.com buying stuff when I should've been working. I would rush through my appointments with off-site clients so I could use the time to go to a store before I had to be back at the office. I started losing business.

"Now I've gotten my spending down to about $600 a month by writing daily goals about not shopping. I limit my time on the Internet to fifteen minutes so I can't online shop as much. It's a constant, daily struggle."

Since shopping guru Paco Underhill has done retail consulting for everyone from McDonald's to Target to Saks, I called him up to find out why, when we run into the mall to get just one thing, we still often emerge with our hands full of bags. What were our favorite stores doing to lure us in, to convince us to buy big?

"Unequivocally, as adults we're responsible for our spending and we ultimately control our own wallets," says Underhill, a disclaimer it sounds like he's repeated many times before. "But stores are working to get you to spend there, and it's more competitive than ever."

Even if you don't notice it, they pump in good smells. "It's a biological function, getting our saliva and glands working. At Williams-Sonoma, there's always potpourri or something cooking." They also corral us on a special path through the store. "Most of us are right-handed, which means your left hand is for holding and your right hand is for grabbing. By circulating us counterclockwise, they ensure you grab the good stuff." They hire nonaggressive greeters who just say "hello" when you walk into a store—but simply by acknowledging you instead of letting you stay anonymous, they make you feel connected to the store. They cluster items—which explains why I often love a sweater and also the bag, pants, flats, camisole, and belt it's displayed with. "They're not trying to sell you one thing—they're trying to sell you a complete look," Underhill explains.

All of those strategies seem intuitive. Then there are the subliminal lures. For example, many stores—he names Gap, Ann Taylor, and Anthropologie specifically—position the sale rack in the back left-hand corner that's visible from the store's entrance. That way, you have to walk through, "getting you as deep in the store as possible." An old dressing room trick, lots of stores now use flattering lighting to make anything look more appealing. "But whether you're buying an apple, a dress, or an appliance, it won't look as good under your lights at home." Finally, there's vanity sizing—where a size 12 dress labeled size 10 (my mom shops at Chico's for its 0/1/2 sizing system, so she knows she'll never be bigger than a 2) makes you feel good, like, " 'Gee, maybe the three trips I've made to the gym this month really worked!' " says Underhill.

I always figured if the time came to cut back on my own spending, I'd just do it, and so would everyone else. Going into the 2008 holiday shopping season, it sounded like that time had come. We were six months into a recession with no end in sight. Fannie Mae and Freddie Mac were in financial ruin, not to mention Lehman Brothers, Bear Stearns, and the Big Three automakers. Stocks had taken the worst plunge in decades, draining our 401(k)s. Layoffs commenced across industries. Morning shows switched from segments on fabulous holiday getaways to ones on budgeting. Fashion magazines focused on "steals" and yanked the $10,000 Vuitton purses or limited the number of "price upon request" items shown per page. The news hammered home the point every night that America was in its worst financial crisis since the Great Depression.

Needless to say, economists thought it would be a bleak season for retailers.

A surprise to everyone—though it shouldn't have been—was that Americans still poured into the malls in droves, credit cards in hand. Despite the financial world crumbling around us, Americans spent 7 percent *more* on 2008's Black Friday than on the same day a year before, when times were relatively flush. The Mall of America alone rang up about $2 billion in sales that year. Was it that we just didn't want to stop shopping, or that we couldn't?

At the Mall of America, you can buy: a white fluffy rug or a white fluffy sweater or a white fluffy pillow or a white fluffy anything at the Alpaca Connection.

At the Mall of America, you can buy: a wedding from the third-floor's Chapel of Love, which seats seventy. Prices range from $299 to $849, which includes one unity candle, two toasting glasses, a garter, and one bottle of champagne. A Minnesota Twins garter is available, as is a vintage-inspired "heirloom hand-kerchief" that says *Grandma* in faded embroidery. Floral packages are extra.

After twenty-four hours of walking, sitting, and eating in the Mall of America, I see each and every one of its 520 stores, facades that span 4.3 indoor miles. I stand on a conveyor belt that pulls me through the world's largest underground aquarium, housed in the mall's basement. The whole MOA complex is always a perfectly comfortable seventy degrees. The mall regulates this by gale force air-conditioning, even in the dead of subzero Minnesota winters, to counter the heat of all of those lights and skylights and all of us shoppers sweating and breathing and buying.

I'm walking around and around the rings of the mall, starting to think of Dante's *Inferno*. Depending on where I am, my thoughts are interrupted by a row of shrieks and chugs from the riders of the roller coaster at Camp Snoopy. Sometimes I stop to take a few notes or eat a hot pretzel or look around at some of the teenage girls and wonder what they're here for, or whether they even know. I wish I had my car here—I do my best thinking when I can put on music I like and open up the engine, as if driving faster helps me zoom by all the ideas that stand in the way of me and an answer.

I decide to park myself on a bench for a few minutes so that my feet will feel less like water balloons and more like feet. The candy shop across the street is buzzing with kids and teenagers, a sugar hive. I see two girls who look about fourteen spooning jelly beans into a paper bag, taking a few out to see if they really do taste like popcorn or strawberry jam.

I am so tired of walking in that slow, shuffling pace required for the mall. I'm tired of seeing grown men in sandals. I'm tired of the same stores over and over, one that sells only socks two doors down from another store that sells only socks. It's hour nineteen in the Mall of America, and I don't have any more answers than when I first walked through the massive row of glass doors to get in here. I'm sick of the mall food, becoming less amused that the California Cafe's "outdoor terrace" overlooks the mall's indoor courtyard, the hanging fake grapes like you're eating inside a diorama.

At the Mall of America, you can buy: a Green Bay Packers Tiffany lamp from a store called Rybicki, which also sells cheese.

What does the future hold for the mall? Underhill says there probably won't ever be another Mall of America–type mall built in America.

"We've reached the apogee of making it bigger," he says.

"Almost all American shopping chains would be immensely healthier if they were smaller. But Wall Street has been asking them to keep expanding. It's the traditional problem in American retail."

Besides, he says, America—inventor and original home of the mall—is far from leading the mall pack these days.

"Most shopping malls in the United States are twenty-five years old [the Mall of America was built in 1992] and they were ugly the day they opened. So the malls that everybody talks about now are the Vasco da Gama Center in Lisbon and the malls in Dubai, Brazil, and Moscow. The places that are leading in malls are places where money is young," says Underhill.

What will our malls look like in the future, then, if not like the Mall of America?

"Almost every developer after 2008 is talking not about malls but about 'alls,' meaning something that has some built-in population density like a hotel, apartment buildings, and commercial office space," he says.

If "alls" sound like an improbable solution, consider that the "all" system has worked in Australia. There, the stores are next to doctors' offices, health clubs, and day care centers, so that their malls really *are* a center of the community, as opposed to just a place for shopping. In Scandinavia, some malls include libraries and schools and churches.

As the big anchor stores close—in 2009, Macy's, Sears, Dillard's, Mervyns, Linens 'n Things, Circuit City, and Steve & Barry's all shuttered some of their mall locations—landlords need to find a way to fill the space. Temporary stores are popping up in malls, and down-market shops, like Big Lots and discount stores, are being offered leases in malls that turned their noses up at these kinds of retailers just a year before. Still, despite letting less-than-desirable companies move in and offering discounted rent to others, storefronts are still dark. "Of all the vacant spaces, the most difficult to fill are anchors—those big stores at the periphery of a mall," says the *New York Times* article "Malls Test Experimental Waters to Fill Vacancies." One solution is for malls to subdivide the giant empty spaces; landlords are taking a now-empty anchor store and putting a Best Buy on one level and a Dick's Sporting Goods on the other.

Malls are also bringing in medical centers, grocery stores, community colleges, dance studios, and even gigantic indoor waverider simulators. For years, we had so many retail stores that we built more and more malls to hold them; now, we're unable to fill what we built and are looking for ways to repurpose these mammoth, mostly impractical spaces. The main problem is that "in this economy, few chains need spaces as large as the ones coming onto the market," according to the *New York Times* story. You could argue that, blinded by a boom in rampant consumerism, we built short-sighted solutions, and now we're paying the price. Or you could argue that we were on a financial upswing for so long that no one could have predicted how quickly a recession could make such structures irrelevant, even burdensome. Either way, we've got the problem of big, empty mall shells.

It became a fatal problem for an American company called General Growth, the country's second-largest mall operator, which manages such shopping meccas as Ala Moana Center in Honolulu, Water Tower Place in Chicago, and the Grand Canal Shoppes at the Venetian in Las Vegas. You've probably shopped in a General Growth mall; they ran more than two hundred properties in forty-four states. Though the company had been around since 1954, they filed for bankruptcy in 2009 in what *The New York Times* called, "one of the biggest commercial real estate collapses in United States history."

General Growth isn't alone, of course. In 2009, the mall vacancy rate hit its highest point in almost a decade. The vacancy rate at the end of 2008 was 7.1 percent, jumping from 5.8 percent a year before. "That has left many of the roughly 1,500 malls in the United States groping for a solution—any solution—to their woes," said the same *New York Times* article. "Some have converted retail space into office space. Others have drastically lowered rents for prized tenants, agreeing to cut deals to keep revenue flowing. Some have simply gone dark."

The question now is what to do with empty malls, and every expert has his own recommendation. Peter Blackbird, founder of the Web site www.deadmalls.com, thinks we should bulldoze them, rather than let them sit vacant. "Although it may be sad to see a place with so many memories bulldozed, there isn't much future for an abandoned generic suburban shopping mall," he says. Especially "if the building is cheaply constructed, and neglected for years, the only viable option is demolition." Communities shouldn't let them sit, he thinks, because a failed mall is "a weight on the community," resulting in "lost tax revenue and jobs, increased vandalism and crime, and lower property values."

By contrast, Joel Kotkin, author of *The City: A Global History*, sees failing malls as "an opportunity for communities." He argues that they can realistically be repurposed into what a community needs, since they have "existing infrastructure and usually are located on major transportation routes." By adding "urban amenities like interesting restaurants, live music and local festivals," he says, we can "retain low-density environments of single-family homes preferred by the vast majority of Americans." Basically, we can offer cool "urban amenities" without requiring people to move out of the suburbs. In that way, a dead mall can enrich our lives.

Ellen Dunham-Jones and June Williamson, authors of *Retrofitting Suburbia: Urban Design Solutions for Redesigning Suburbs,* also see the upshot in the collapse of big malls. "While no one likes to see businesses fail, dead malls provide great opportunities for communities to redevelop in healthy ways," they write. The two think abandoned malls can even help us go green. "Many malls, especially in the Northeast and Midwest, were built on large wetlands before those sites were environmentally protected," they point out. "The death of those malls will provide an opportunity to repair the regional landscape by turning them back to open space." It all sounded a little pie in the sky to me. Other than as the setting for some postapocalyptic movie, I couldn't imagine us turning our commercial spaces back over to nature. But Dunham-Jones and Williamson point to places where it's already happened, like "the restored wetlands that replaced a strip shopping center in Phalen," a neighborhood of Saint Paul, Minnesota.

It's clear that big malls are in trouble, making construction of big new malls a fairly glaring bad idea. No new enclosed malls have opened in the U.S. since 2006. No surprise, considering right now Americans can't afford to buy big enough to support them. Regardless, construction is under way in East Rutherford, New Jersey, on the country's biggest mall, one that would easily eclipse the MOA. It's been stalled by the recession, thanks to its $2 billion price tag. But if it's completed as planned, this Xanadu will include a skydiving simulator, an indoor wave pool, and a Ferris wheel, plus hundreds of storefronts.

*   *   *

I'm still walking around the Mall of America, circling like a buzzard, spinning my imaginary wheels. Then I walk by A.C.E.S., a virtual reality arcade. I figure that after twenty-four hours at the mall, I can't get any less tethered to reality, so I may as well keep moving away from it.

Once I buy my ticket and get behind the wheel of a NASCAR simulation game (at the Mall of America, you can buy a $15 virtual flying or driving experience), I'm cruising. My seat bucks and rumbles when I veer too far off the road, and I jam the plastic accelerator to the floor. It becomes clear that I've accidentally selected to drive on a racetrack instead of what I meant to pick, a straight shot along the shoreline. So I go around and around in circles, not able to change a thing, a sensation that feels all too familiar.

9.
ALL WRAPPED UP IN DEBT

'm driving an actual car today, going eighty-five miles an hour in a rental, zooming through the tiny roads that wind alongside the cornfields of Minnesota, a few hours away from the Mall of America. The air is hot, and the windows are down. My hair whips around my face, sticking to the sweat on the back of my neck. The radio out here mostly plays patriotic country music, but we gave up on music an hour ago. Now we just fume in silence, punctuated by screaming about mile markers and speed traps and who has to pee. I'm on a road trip with my mother, the kind that you set out upon because you think it will further cement your bond with someone, will remind you exactly why you love each other, but really ends up reminding you of why you make each other nuts.

We need to get to our destination soon, or else the next time we stop for a soda, only one of us is getting back into the car. Sweat seals our backs to the car seats, and there's nothing around us but field after field. We still haven't found what we're after, the world's largest ball of twine—but that's probably for the best because any twine we could find at this point we'd likely use to strangle each other.

I've got to admit, I will pretty much stop at the biggest *anything,* even if it's something I see constantly and am not impressed by at home when it's regular size: rosebushes, pizza, rubber bands. But when I'm driving past the biggest one or biggest collection of these mundane things, I can't resist, my left hand gravitating toward the turn signal, my passengers groaning.

On childhood car trips, my dad would pull over at every historic battle marker sign, every scenic overlook, every single dinky railroad or baseball or Civil War museum—he'd probably be here with us if he didn't have to work this week. My dad's pit stops always annoyed me, and I'd usually try to distract him with deep conversation, hoping he wouldn't notice the upcoming exit sign. I'd let him go on for breathless stretches about the time Question Mark and the Mysterians stayed in his friend's college dorm room, and how he had to eat a squirrel just to be polite when he worked in rural Tennessee for AmeriCorps, and how, when he went for his first real job interview, he was living in a tent with my mom, looping his tie into a half-Windsor while trying to cook oatmeal on a camp stove. Though he'd told me these same stories so often that I could recite them, I stayed silent. This usually worked for two to three historic landmarks, but eventually the spell of nostalgia always lifted, and we'd pull over to read some rusted sign stuck just off the shoulder about the Civil War spot where Confederate General Gideon J. Pillow surrendered.

Clearly an obsession with roadside attractions runs in the family. Today, however, I've taken my fixation to another level. In fact, I plotted this *entire trip* around one. The ball of twine is not a silly pit stop on the way to somewhere else; it's the destination.

Francis A. Johnson, the man who made the twine ball, has been dead for almost twenty years. To some, his bizarre life's work may seem a waste of time, but I'm fascinated. Maybe it's because the twine ball means something else, a physical embodiment of a life dedicated to preparedness. Johnson survived the Great Depression, his compulsive collecting—of twine and many other common items—a lingering survival skill. It's totally possible the guy was just plain bonkers, as my mom firmly believes. But it seemed to me, from a hundred years and several thousand miles away, that maybe Johnson was onto something, that he'd come out of the Depression with some kind of insurance plan that, if it wasn't a practical, tangible help, could at least be an emotional salve. As the nightly news whipped up fear that we were heading into the Great Depression II and I felt completely unprepared for what that might mean or how I might deal with it, I needed to know if a giant ball of twine, and the man who created it, might provide me with some guidance.

Johnson was born in 1904. While most people expect their twenties and thirties to be the start of their financial independence, Johnson found himself financially decimated by the Great Depression. Rural areas, like the part of Minnesota where he lived, were hit especially hard, with crop prices sinking by 40 to 60 percent. Johnson learned about fluctuations the hard way. Even after the Depression, while most people celebrated, he spent his life preparing for the day when America wouldn't be on top again.

Since childhood, the idea of America crashing down from its perch as the world's most dominant country, both in terms of economy and military, has absolutely terrified and fascinated me. I wondered what it would be like for kids my same age who were growing up in countries that weren't full of power and plenty, where the economy had collapsed, the country was being invaded, or people stood in lines for food or gasoline (I didn't learn about America's own rationing until I was in high school), making those places seem like some faraway, unstable "other." I was taught in school and generally informed by the culture that America was the

best place in the world to live, definitely because of our democracy
and freedom, but also because we were the richest—and as a result, most powerful—place in the Western world. And though that
kind of nationalistic thinking was probably supposed to make me
feel grateful and secure as an elementary-aged American, it also left
me considering the contrary: *if we weren't always the richest and most
powerful, doesn't that mean we may not be again?* I dealt with the ter-
ror I felt at that idea by simply banishing it from my mind, until
growing economies in places like China and Japan made it impossible to keep ignoring. So when the economy imploded in 2008,
resulting in the worst period of foreclosures, debts, and bankruptcies since the Great Depression, and leaving much of American
industry leaning on the (cash-strapped) U.S. government for bail-
outs, I felt compelled to see the product of someone else's idea of
readiness. Even if no one else saw it that way, to me it was the
world's largest monument to financial self-reliance.

It was time to go to the twine ball.

Today, more Americans than ever before—60 percent of us—
carry credit card debt. We also owe more than ever before. The
average owed on credit cards in 1990 was $2,900; by 2007, it had
skyrocketed to more than $8,000. For someone who owes $10,000,
it will take 57.5 years of paying the minimum balance before they're
in the black. Even more bleak, 13 percent of the people who have
balances on their credit cards owe $25,000 or more (which means,
by the time it's finally paid off in minimum-payment increments,
it will have cost an extra $58,932 in interest). Annually, more than
nine billion credit card offers are mailed out. That's about thirty
cards per American per year, without even mentioning the stories
we've all heard about the family pet receiving a credit card ap-

plication. And though of course not all of those are activated, the average American does carry four credit cards.

Finally hitting some nonfield scenery, my mother and I drive past brown and dusty white horses, a coffee shop called Latte Da, and a combination carwash/gas station/dog bathing place. We pass Jack's bar, boasting Grain Belt beer, and a sign that says, IF YOU LIVED IN DARWIN, YOU'D BE HOME NOW.

We finally turn into Darwin, a 252-person town with two bars plus a liquor store. We make a left onto what our map calls County Road 14, but the street sign calls 1st Street. Farther to the left, we spot the water tower, and in front of it, a sign for the twine ball; we are saved. During the lost, loopy, detour-riddled drive, we've been looking forward to dinner at the Twine Ball Inn, its claim to fame being that its windows overlook the eponymous landmark. Since there are no hotels in Darwin, we figured we'd fill up on burgers and fries in Darwin's only restaurant before heading back to Minneapolis. But as we cruise by the inn, we see a sign painted by a brevity-obsessed plans spoiler: CLD. RMODELG. My mother and I turn to look at each other with a face that says: this is all your fault.

"Remind me, why do you need to come here again?" she asks, not really asking.

"To see the twine ball."

"Right. And why do you need to see the twine ball?"

But I can't think of an answer, and when someone who gave birth to you is making that tired, expectant face, you want to have an earnest answer for her.

A few weeks before, I sat down with my friend Julia to play her favorite childhood board game. It's called Barbie Queen of the

Prom, and is made by Mattel. Growing up, she'd played her mother's 1961 version, so Julia was the first one to run to a toy store in 2006, when Mattel reissued a "faithful reproduction" of the original game. The goals in Barbie's life—and yours, as the young female players—were obviously, if not hysterically, antiquated. To be the winner, which means being crowned prom queen, you must nab a steady boyfriend, a pretty prom gown, and get elected president of one of the school's clubs. It was easy enough for us, women who grew up in the era of Title IX and Madonna, to laugh at how obviously times had changed for the better. *Look at how backward they were back then—we're so much more enlightened now!* We clinked our wineglasses and sat down at Julia's coffee table to play.

Once we got to the section where we could buy our prom dresses, though, we hit a snag: the dresses were $65 and neither of us had anything close to that in our modest stack of play money. Simple, we figured—charge it! We'd just use the game's credit vouchers and pay it back to the bank later on, when we'd passed a few more payment squares (by doing the dishes, collecting allowance, or doing calligraphy). The problem was, though, that the bank only offered $40 in credit vouchers, *total*, for everyone to share.

"Um, how am I supposed to get the dress I want?" I said.

It's embarrassing to admit it now, but for a moment we looked at each other, completely baffled. Was this game defective, missing pieces? Were we just short a few vouchers?

It took a moment to sink in.

"I guess you don't get a dress until you can afford it," Julia said. "Harsh."

We certainly hadn't planned on any generational financial epiphanies coming from a few glasses of Riesling and a Barbie board game, but here we were. It had become clear in an instant the difference in financial principles of players in 1961 (earn, save, plan, then buy) and of us modern players (buy now, pay later).

We sat around for another hour or so to finish playing the game, but something about it had stopped being so funny.

My mom and I climb out of the car, stooped, with knees cracking. In an octagonal Plexiglas enclosure topped by a wood roof, we can make out the outline, but the glare obscures the details. I fast-walk toward it, trying not to seem too eager, but I'm bursting. I can't wait to see what twenty-nine consecutive years of work looks like. I'm not even twenty-nine years old, and dedicating yourself to a single project for that long seems impossible. The twine ball is a physical and real and tangible product of a life's work, of someone dedicated—maybe compulsively so—to saving scraps I wouldn't think twice about throwing away.

It's only closer, once I've gotten past the angle of the glare, with my face and hands pressed up on the glass, that I can see the details. Francis A. Johnson's bailout plan is real and indisputable, because it weighs 17,400 pounds. It is eleven feet high. It is forty feet around. He worked on it for four hours a day, every day, for those twenty-nine years. He didn't need to borrow anything. He didn't take more than he needed. And he certainly didn't waste.

An older lady in pink sweatpants and with gray frizzy hair toddles over toward me. I think she's going to scold me for leaving palm- and nose-prints on the glass, but instead, she seems personally flattered by my interest. She is Thea, the volunteer on duty today in the Twine Ball Museum, a trailerlike building behind the twine ball gazebo.

"What does it smell like?" I say. "Is it falling apart in the middle? How long will it last for? Tell me everything."

Thea smiles and pulls a key from a band around her wrist. She opens the Plexiglas door and gestures for me to go inside.

The Great Depression eventually eased up, but Johnson still couldn't get past his Depression-era mind-set. He became a collector, holding on to things. I wonder if it's because he went through a time when you couldn't count on anyone else—even institutions we're asked to implicitly trust for their stability, like banks and the government—to be there and give you what you need, so you start making your own plan. Johnson started keeping everything: pencil nubs, nails, pieces of string. "Don't throw anything out" was the message—you might need it again, and then who are you gonna ask for it? How are you going to buy and provide when the banks and the stock market lose your money? So Johnson saved, an act that showed his wariness about the future, an act of fear and cynicism. Or else it was an act of personal responsibility, heroic and independent.

Either way, the Depression made Johnson decide to stop relying on anyone else to cover his needs—no FDIC, no food stamps, no farm equipment stores or dime stores. He would save everything so that one day he'd have pencils for his kids to write their homework with, and he'd have twine to rope up the bales of hay to feed his animals, not counting on anyone else to get him what he needed. He may have wondered, why throw out the pieces of string every time you cut off an extra section, and then later run out of string and have to buy more? Why not just save the excess you have, not depend on others, be more self-reliant, save instead of purge? Stuff, even small stuff like golf pencils, had importance to him, potential future worth. Johnson's passion wasn't necessarily a passion at all, but perhaps a compulsive defense plan.

And it wasn't just rural farmers like Johnson who went into collector mode during or after the Depression. Even J. Paul Getty, fellow Minnesotan and benefactor to the Getty art museum in Los Angeles (and one of the first individuals to make a billion dollars), was known to force houseguests in his mansion to use a pay phone. One of the richest men in the country, who was so moneyed that he retired in 1917 at twenty-five years old, became a "pathological cheapskate" who even "squirreled away bits of string to later re-use." Though he didn't roll them into a ball, he kept those pieces of string, waiting for the day he might not be the richest man in the richest country in the world.

Today, most Americans—myself included—aren't much like Johnson. We're not saving. In fact, we now have the lowest rate of savings in the Western world. In 2005, 2006, and 2007, our savings rate was *negative* for the first time in American history other than 1932 and 1933, during the heart of the Great Depression.

In part, Americans can justify relying so heavily on credit because our government does the same. Living in New York, I sometimes walk by the National Debt Clock in Times Square. The numbers spin by on digital squares unreadably fast, spinning like a slot machine before it renders its verdict. The clock was put up in 1989 to record our then-debt, $2.7 trillion, and has been spinning ever since. But in October 2008, the debt outdid the clock, spinning beyond thirteen digits. That month, the national debt exceeded $10 trillion. In 2009, just twenty years after it was erected, the National Debt Clock added two more digits so that the clock will one day be able to chart a quadrillion—yes, that's a real number—dollars of our debt.

The U.S. government racks up $1 trillion annually in debt. So where does that money come from? Around that much is collected every year in taxes, but that's not the only place the government collects from. According to the Treasury Department, in September of 2008, China became America's largest foreign creditor and, says *The Washington Post,* China "may be the government's largest creditor, period." As of fall 2008, we owed that country nearly $800 billion, which accounts for 10 percent of our country's total debt. Japan, whom we used to owe the most to, now credits us $573 billion, less than China for the first time in U.S. history. Don't worry—there's a cap on how much the government can borrow from the public, including foreign creditors, limited to only $12.1 trillion.

Who we're in debt to has an immense impact on the prosperity—and safety—of our nation. The article notes, "In contrast to Japan, one of the United States' closest allies, China is seen as less benevolent to U.S. interests." America owing to China raises several concerns, including possibly "jeopardizing Washington's ability to fund a stimulus package to jump-start the economy, quickly raising interest rates on a variety of loans in the U.S." and making it "harder for U.S. companies to sell their products overseas." When our government is willing to spend, regardless of the cost, isn't it easy to play fast and loose ourselves?

When I step inside the gazebo, the twine ball towers over me, double my height. The rope is sisal, the technical name for baling twine. It's fraying and shaggy from knots. The room feels humid, like a terrarium, on my bare arms. The air smells like wet hay, musty in a different way than a grandmother's attic smells, but musty in that all-weather smell of a country barn. I do a quick check to see whether Thea, the twine ball tour guide/guard, is watching. She's talking to my mom about the guest book and trying to sell her on a twine ball bumper sticker—mug combo on sale inside. I take this as my chance and reach out my hand, rest it palm-open against the ball. It's so densely packed it hardly gives, not at all the spongy mass I thought it'd be. I think about what would happen if I pulled one of the strings, whether it might roll away and unravel, unfurling all of its 1,144 miles. I run my finger along a single dreadlocked strand, dirty blond and strong, as if woven from the hair of Samson.

I imagine Francis A. Johnson running his hands over a piece of twine in exactly the same way. It was 1950, and he was still living in Meeker, the rural Minnesota county where he was born. His neighbors described him as a serious man who kept to himself. He didn't have children or a wife, and at forty-six years old, it didn't look like he would get either soon. He may have felt that he already disappointed his father, U.S. Senator Magnus Johnson, the country's first immigrant senator. With so much to live up to, and with such a disheartening result, Johnson might have been looking for a passion, too, a way to define himself. As a boy, he worked as a farmhand, and grew up to be a self-employed carpenter, always working with his hands. So maybe he was just looking for something to keep his idle fingers busy on that day in March 1950, when he first wrapped some baler twine around two fingers, and the next day, just kept going.

Johnson was always a collector. In addition to those small golf pencils, he collected hundreds of rusty old padlocks and pens, even if they were dried up. He kept more than a thousand keys in a box next to his fifteen poppy seed grinders. He stored more than a thousand wrenches for no obvious reason. He collected nails of all different sizes and so many nail aprons—1,700 of them, all hung up in a row—that they were purchased by Ripley's Believe It or Not after his death. The collections were so varied that it seemed the only important thing, the only thing he was amassing, was more collections.

Who knows—maybe he just had an undiagnosed case of obsessive-compulsive disorder. But I wondered if maybe he had a few lessons to teach those of us who are struggling today.

Every day, for four hours, Johnson looked out onto the same pastoral expanse that's now in front of me, and wound pieces of twine in a circle. He wrapped the ball until he needed to lift it with a crane, a huge railroad jack designed to lift boxcars, in order to keep on wrapping. For the next twenty-nine years, he wound the twine ball, until one day in 1979, he was done. Not a talkative man, Johnson never explained why he stopped—whether it was a matter of physics, or that he'd reached some kind of serene mental stasis and felt finished. *Guinness World Records* came and catalogued it, naming it the World's Largest Ball of Twine. Then Ripley's came calling, offering Johnson enough money to start a new collection of gold-plated shoes if he'd wanted. They would move the ball to their museum, and Johnson would likely never see it again. But he wanted the rest of the world to know about the hometown he loved, and the twine ball was—and still is—Darwin's only tourist attraction. So he refused to sell.

For the first few years, Johnson kept the twine ball chained to a tree in his front lawn. Though he kept it on his property, at one point he moved it to an open-air shed. Johnson refused to put it in a locked enclosure, the way it sits today, thinking it belonged to everyone. Everyone seemed to think it belonged to them, too; visitors or townies frequently stopped to snip off a piece as a souvenir. They wanted a piece of the magic, or the kitsch, or the spectacle, or a little snippet to hold in their hands and imagine what that kind of emergency preparedness must feel like.

Other people took notice of Ripley's offers, though, and weren't as impressed by Johnson's refusal to cash in. Texan J. C. Payne constructed the new world's largest twine ball in 1987, which replaced Johnson's in *Guinness* just two years before he died. Though Johnson didn't seem openly upset about losing the twine ball title, Darwin rallied, pointing out the flaws in Payne's system: he used an army of other people, and used "twine" made of synthetic colored nylon rather than real baling twine. In order to keep their "world's largest" title, the Community Club (run by volunteers like Thea) began labeling Johnson's creation as the World's Largest Ball of Twine Made by One Man, an addendum many others in Darwin think is insulting.

In the early 1990s, representatives from Ripley came back to Darwin. Maybe they figured that since Johnson had been dead a few years, the Community Club would cave. Thea says that Ripley's kept asking, "Who's going to see it in Darwin?" but the club upheld Johnson's wishes and wouldn't sell. Instead, they sold his nail apron collection, and used the money to move the twine ball into a protective gazebo off Darwin's main street, to make signs and a museum staffed by Community Club volunteers in the summers. Would Johnson approve of the bumper sticker–mug combo my mom is currently buying, along with my two magnets and a button? Likely not. But can you blame us for wanting a piece of what one man considered his handmade insurance policy?

* * *

In close-knit communities across America, people have been buying things from the country store "on credit" for at least a hundred years. But getting something before you paid for it—especially if you weren't personally known by your creditor—didn't really exist until 1959, when the first credit cards were issued by BankAmericard, which later became Visa. Still, charging didn't become widespread until the mid-1990s, when additional cards, such as American Express and Discover, also began letting consumers carry a balance from month to month.

"Both lenders and borrowers abused the system," says Farnoosh Torabi, author of *You're So Money: Live Rich, Even When You're Not*. "It was easy to overborrow. American debt is largely a result of the infiltration of credit cards, combined with our 'bigger is better' and 'bling it on' general cultural attitude. We are a nation of bulk shoppers, McMansion inhabitants, and Super Big Gulp Diet Coke slurpers. As a result, we have spent beyond our means for twenty-five years now. Societal pressures to live certain lifestyles—to live in certain neighborhoods, drive certain cars and dress a certain way—lead many to want to overspend, and the *way* they can overspend is through credit cards. Plastic lets us immediately satisfy our wants without paying for them right away."

It's no surprise, then, that we're completely credit card saturated. In 2006, the Census Bureau found that there were nearly 1.5 billion credit cards in use in the United States. A stack of all those credit cards would be taller than a dozen Mount Everests. There are, however, a few definite perks to having credit cards. Some consumers like the convenience of not having to carry cash; others point out benefits like cash back or points for products or airline travel. But in exchange for these benefits, the majority is being charged ever more in late fees and interest; according to the Government Accountability Office, the average credit card late payment fee jumped 115 percent from 1995 to 2005. It also means, based upon Federal Reserve figures, Americans owe a staggering total of $750 to $800 billion on credit card balances.

Other stats show that between the multiple credit cards, the average American has access to approximately $19,000 in loans, making it no wonder that carrying a balance of a few thousand doesn't seem like the end of the world. But it's not just that credit cards give us access to money we don't have—they actually entice us to spend more, since people who use credit cards spend a full 20 percent more than those who make their purchases in cash, according to the National Foundation for Credit Counseling. College students are carrying record-high credit card balances, an average of $3,173; as of 2009, 21 percent of undergrads carried balances of between $3,000 and $7,000, according to Sallie Mae.

Knowing all of this, what are we supposed to do? I certainly don't plan on winding my own ball of twine or collecting broken pencils so that I'll never have to buy a writing utensil again.

"We need to be more fearful of debt," says Torabi. "If we think of debt as financial imprisonment, which it absolutely is, perhaps we'd be more responsible with our money. The recent recession has made more people afraid of debt because many of us finally saw or experienced the consequences firsthand—when your house gets taken away, when you can't get a job because your credit report stinks, when you have to close your small business because you can't pay your bills, debt becomes much more than a four-letter word. It becomes a force we finally have to reckon with."

It sounds like doomsday. "But that's actually been a good thing," argues Torabi. "We're at the beginning of a financial revolution. I'm hoping it will motivate people to learn the fundamentals of financial independence: set both short- and long-term goals, be conscious of how much money you earn and how much money you spend, save often and regularly, and be your biggest financial advocate."

Inside the museum are signs telling me to HAVE A BALL IN DARWIN! and seemingly a million different colored shirts with the outline of Minnesota and a big twine ball to mark Darwin. The walls are plastered with newspaper articles from the town's history. I learn that when Johnson was in school, he might've called his love interest a "sweet patula," and danced with her to the music of the Sod Busters. That the cheerleaders in his high school wore white polo shirts, dark slacks, white frilly socks, and shiny Mary Janes. That a front-page story in the local newspaper in 1952 was not about Winston Churchill announcing England had an atomic bomb, or the publication of *Anne Frank: The Diary of a Young Girl*, or that doctors were performing the first open-heart surgery less than two hundred miles from his home. Instead, the front-page stories he saw were about people like Luke Casey, a 340-pound mail carrier, under the headline: MINNESOTA'S LARGEST POSTMASTER?

In photographs, where even the unhappiest of lips tend to curl into smiles, Johnson looks stern, sad. In both of the most-published pictures of him, Johnson's standing with his arm against the twine ball, leaning on it as if for support. His baggy, weathered overalls cuff at the bottom, and the brim of his baseball cap matches his mouth—a perfectly flat line. It makes me wonder again about what motivated Johnson's idea of preparedness—was it simple pessimism?

The twine ball has brought more than three thousand visitors to Darwin, and those are just the ones who signed the guest book. When Johnson died and a couple moved into his former home, they were shocked by how many strangers they found in their front yard, stopping to see the twine ball, which was a large part of the impetus to move the ball into town. The twine ball, it seemed, had its own magnetic force, pulling in curious visitors who had never been haunted by Depression-era memories.

I also can't stop thinking about a friend whom I talked to before I left for Darwin. I told her about why I wanted to see the twine ball, and she didn't get why it meant something to me as more than just another weird roadside attraction. When I start talking about debt and self-sufficiency, she clammed up, abruptly changing the subject by grabbing for a Thai takeout menu and asking what we were ordering for dinner. She's your classic ab-fab New Yorker— midtwenties, immaculately dressed, with a posh apartment, a constant mani-pedi-highlights-blowout, and who was always meeting up after work at the hippest bars for a few $12 cocktails. Since we worked in the same industry, I knew roughly how small her salary must be, so I'd just assumed she was still being supported by family money. But after we called the place to order dinner, she hung up the phone, turning to me as if in confession, and said, "I'm in debt."

"Sure," I said, trying to hide my surprise. "Lots of people are. Especially at our age, and especially living in New York."

"Yeah, but I'm $20,000 in debt," she said, explaining that though a percentage of that was student loans (often considered "good debt," in the same category as mortgages), most were credit card purchases she'd rung up to maintain her girl-on-the-go lifestyle, even after she'd taken a pay cut. "I didn't want to have to give anything up," she said, "and as long as I can keep charging, I don't have to."

My mom stands at the cash register of the gift shop, buying a bumper sticker from Thea. I think of the back of my father's now-retired minivan, decoupaged in THIS CAR CLIMBED PIKE'S PEAK–type stickers, a memory from each of our family's enforced historical landmark tours. I think his bumper stickers were all about pride, happy to show that he was a liberal and a traveler and a man who supported the National Zoo and spawned an honor roll student and a Boy Scout, the kind of man who thought we should all VOTE DEMOCRAT! and GIVE PEAS A CHANCE.

Maybe with all of my dad's roadside stops, he was trying to tell my younger brother and me something: there's an America that existed before us, and there's an America that will exist after us. To give us a sense of history and continuum. To remind us that people once thought Ulysses S. Grant was a god. It's a reminder that the way things are now are not necessarily the way things always will be.

Once in awhile, I feel panic-stricken that I am not as self-reliant as I should be, if at all. If the markets continue to worsen, and the 2008 recession turns into a 2015 depression, I wouldn't know how to save or ration; the way I've lived up until this point has allowed me to forget those virtues, or to never learn them in the first place. Previous generations seem far better equipped to endure discomfort, while I'm part of a coddled generation known for crying if we don't get participation trophies. Maybe we would all toughen up and learn how to cope, but the twine ball brings up all of these uncomfortable reminders, and it's been a long day. My mom and I say good-bye to Thea and get her directions to a nearby restaurant.

There are more waitresses than customers, and we're sitting here eating pulled pork barbecue and slices of fruit pie that taste like butter and sweet melting cherries. I start to worry about how much less independent and knowledgeable my generation is than Johnson's. For example, I don't know how to cook more than two things that are not microwave-ready; I recently had to Google how to make hard-boiled eggs. I don't know how to repair my vacuum cleaner, my TV; when something stops working, my solution is usually just to buy a new one. The limits to my resourcefulness are having my AAA card with me when I get a flat tire and knowing which Thai restaurant near me has the best cheap takeout. Even for things I do know how to fix, like those home ec staples of sewing on a button or fixing a rip on a shirt if it's on a hem, are things I've convinced myself I don't have time for; I either scrap the item or pay a tailor to repair it for me. When I did end up sewing a button on a cardigan earlier this year, I commended myself like I was some brave, resourceful pioneer woman who'd just survived crossing the country in a Conestoga wagon. (The whole time I was using my $2.99 CVS sewing kit, I kept thinking, *Look at me—I'm mending!*) When I showed my handiwork to my friends, they too oohed and aahed like I'd churned my own butter. When I told my grandmother, a survivor of the Great Depression, and my mother, a child of that generation, they both looked at me as if to say, So what? But for me, fixing something myself, even as small as a button, stood for the same thing as the twine ball: I was not used to bailing myself out. I was so not used to it, in fact, that I'd begun to doubt that I even could.

I clink my fork down on the plate, stuffed. When your job is as intangible as turning ideas into words, the concreteness of the twine ball is appealing, both for its solidity and sheer physical staying power. That thing is a monument to Johnson's expertise in scrimping and saving, while the only monument I have to show right now is the swell of receipts in my wallet from this trip. I pick up my fork again, but I get the same feeling I did at the end of the Barbie Prom Queen board game, and suddenly the sweetness of cherries is turning my stomach.

My mom and I get into the car for the long drive back to the city with the Mall of America. As the sun sets orange and pink, I start thinking about trust, and more specifically how my indifference to the values of self-reliance and frugality is an act of faith, a belief in the permanence of the status quo: there will always be a restaurant nearby that will supply me with food when I can't be bothered to make something myself; places will always take credit cards when I don't have cash; there will always be some bank that will give me a loan. But I know it's a specious faith, an ostrich with its head in the sand. It's believing that our economy and our industries are made of resilient Nerf and not handblown glass, assuming that no matter how much pressure we put on them, America will always bounce back securely into its original shape.

We drive past the cornfields until we get to roads packed with cars. While I stare off at the yellow dotted line, my mom reads *Real Simple,* a magazine that represents a movement to declutter, decrap, get rid of the stuff we've accumulated, and generally pare down our lives. For me and others, our stuff is an insurance policy.

Francis Johnson knew that the systems so many of us take for granted aren't permanent; the economy is dynamic, sometimes in ways that are unpleasant (see your 401[k], for instance). Even when those systems feel like they've gone totally bust, as they did during the Depression, eventually they're reconstructed to make the America that my mom and I live in. We stop at the drugstore up the street from our hotel to buy aloe gel for our sunburn and Tums for our cherry pie–induced heartburn, a few magazines to read so we won't get bored, some bottles of water for the hotel room. As I watch my mom hand the salesclerk her credit card, I think about Francis Johnson's collections. To him, I think they were a way to prepare for the inevitable crash, a kind of glue to hold himself together should another financial disaster follow the first.

I hope when that day comes, the world's Francis Johnsons will still accept American Express.

IO.

THIS LANDFILL ISN'T A DUMP

I wouldn't know that Puente Hills of Whittier, California, were mountains of trash if I hadn't already been given reason to suspect it. Sprawling over 1,365 acres, Puente Hills Sanitary Landfill is America's largest in operation. In Florida, which is mostly at sea level, the hills made of buried trash covered in dirt, such as Miami-Dade's "Mount Trashmore," are obvious because they're such geographic anomalies. But here, just sixteen miles outside of downtown Los Angeles, a mountain covered in dry brush and chaparral blends right in. On a smoggy June day, I'm getting a landfill tour from Joe Haworth, an environmental engineer who has spent his career doing PR for Puente Hills and has been dubbed "the high priest of trash." Joe drives us up the windy dirt road to the top of the mountain in an ancient Cadillac Eldorado. I'm surprised by how pastoral and scenic the largest landfill in the country is. I'm astounded by how much the air smells like nothing, like breathing inside an empty bottle. The ground has a squishy sort of give from all the layers of trash. Light brown dirt spreads in every direction. It is lonesome and still at this time of morning without another person in sight. Joe reminds me that this bucolic mountain hideaway is made up of waste from me and people like me: the Happy Meal remnants I threw out on the way to meet up with him, my gum wrappers, and the heaps of paper from earlier drafts of this very same chapter.

At the top of a hill in the distance, about two hundred yards away from the mound Joe and I are standing on, I see where they're burying my garbage. The ground is monochromatic brown as far as I can see, built into perfect little hills, not the rainbow of miscellaneous waste I'd imagined. Joe says I'm standing on top of one hundred million tons of buried trash. It is a number your brain tries to skip right over to avoid grappling with. So he says it again: one hundred millions tons.

One hundred millions tons weighs more than 444,000 Statues of Liberty. And Puente Hills is just one of the 188 landfills in California alone (admittedly, a very large one). Under my feet could be thwarted attempts at screenplays, or the Hollywood star they thought better of giving to Gilbert Godfrey. Joe says that at the very bottom, four hundred feet beneath my dusty sneakers, are newspapers from 1968. That means headlines about Boeing 747's maiden flight, the first 911 emergency telephone system going into service, and the now-infamous photograph of Nguyen Ngoc Loan, a South Vietnamese general, holding a gun to the head of a Vietcong officer the moment before execution. Turns out, I'm standing on a mountain of history—though perhaps the history we don't care to remember.

Joe is ready to stop worrying about garbage. He recently retired after working for the Sanitation Districts of Los Angeles County for thirty years, an area generating 30,000 tons of solid waste every day. Joe cares deeply about trash—how we make it and what should happen to it. To him, the biggest struggle L.A. faces may not be gang violence or underfunded school systems, but garbage, the problem everyone contributes to but no one wants to deal with. That's part of why he comes back—to give people like me a tour, to check in with his former assistant, who took Joe's old seat. The same way we can't stop filling the landfill, Joe can't stop coming to it.

The average American produces about 4.8 pounds of garbage a day. That's a 1,752-pound pile of trash from every person, every year. I'm no exception. Maybe it's because I occasionally buy individually packaged juice boxes and those variety packs of sugary cereal boxes; packaging makes up nearly one-third of America's trash. Or how I throw out an empty soda can if there's not a recycling bin nearby, which wastes as much energy as if that can was half filled with gasoline. And Americans throw out enough office paper each year to make a twelve-foot "great wall of paper" from New York to Los Angeles. Per capita, the folks of Indiana generate the most trash, a staggering 2.1 tons per person per year. South Dakotans generate the least, at 0.7 tons.

Across the country, it's an American ritual: once or twice a week, we wrap all of our brightly colored, stinky garbage into a plastic bag that will take up to 1,000 years to decompose, and we put it on the curb for someone else to take away. When I do it, I don't especially think about where that trash goes. At most, I wonder for a minute, *Are they still burning it? What about dumping it in the ocean or shooting it into space?* It's a problem that goes away, far from my hypothetical backyard. So here, in Puente Hills Sanitary Landfill, Joe Haworth stands, among my Lucky Charms boxes and Coke cans and plastic bags.

He tells me that there are only two man-made things visible from space. One is the Great Wall of China. The other is—at one time the largest dump in the world, now closed—Fresh Kills Landfill in Staten Island. Though the New York government and several schools of landscape architecture insist it's visible from the moon, NASA won't confirm it. Joe is convinced it is, and that's part of what's worrying him.

"I'm not angry anymore," he says. "I can't stay at that level of anger without giving in to some level of resignation."

He certainly doesn't look the part of a disgruntled citizen. With his short-sleeve, middle-management dress shirt, L.A. Sanitation District baseball cap, thick-lens glasses that make his brown eyes seem even wider than they are, and a "What's up, Doc?" Warner Brothers tie bumping out like a roller coaster over his round belly, he surely doesn't give off a caustic, rancorous look. Nor does the booming, announcerlike voice in which he makes his corny asides.

"See that sign for 'Clean Dirt'? It's my favorite oxymoron," he says.

Joe laughs at his own jokes. I'm surprised at how lighthearted he can be after cleaning up after our collective mess, every day waking up and knowing that our garbage will become his. When he talks of the future, it's not a vision of his own perfect post-retirement life, lounging on a beach chair, peach daiquiri in hand. No, Joe's thinking of a world in which someone else—ideally, everyone else—will share a little bit of the burden. Though it's something pretty basic, he wants it badly enough for me to know it's important.

"Basically, there are three kinds of people in the population," he says. "A third of them will recycle no matter what because they care about the planet and want to do the right thing. A third will recycle if you make it easy enough for them, give the right incentives, make sure they have color-coded bins and all that. And a third won't do it no matter what, because they think we're a bunch of Commies and recycling is some big hippie conspiracy."

Joe finds it hard to talk to the last group. After spending thirty years in the Main Information Office building, across from the country's largest landfill, he is well aware of the disconnect some people have between the trash they produce and that same trash's impact on the earth. Will we ever learn? I'm starting to understand the impact of my trash, but will it mean that ultimately I will produce any less of it?

The dump is not, technically, a dump. Puente Hills is a "sanitary landfill," which means the trash is buried every single day by a foot of dirt and recycled organic materials, like lawn clippings and mulch. A sign in the lobby of Joe's building touts Puente Hills as a "modern metropolitan landfill"; this euphemistic turn of phrase makes the place sound more like an art museum than a pile of Los Angeles trash. But when I stood with Joe on top of the four-hundred-foot mountain made of garbage, I was surprised to find that Puente Hills looked more like several uniformly brown hills and canyons than a mound of putrefying, roach-and-rat-infested trash.

I'd brought a bandanna with me to tie around my nose, Wild West–style, in case the stench was unbearable. Imagining the sweet wet-rot smell of my own 33.6 pounds of weekly garbage, I couldn't begin to imagine how pungent this would be on a macro level. Joe keeps the windows up while we drive through the landfill, and I assume this is so I won't gag; I can practically imagine the wavy green stink lines undulating from the ground. When Joe pulls over on the top of our mountain and suggests we walk around, I open the door tentatively, holding my breath.

But once I see spots and exhale, I'm shocked. The air smells like . . . well, like air. The ground looks like a construction site. There's nothing to hear but the gentle hum of machines pushing dirt and packing down trash in the distance. There's nothing to see but plain dirt mountains, uniform swirls of dirt for acres in every direction. It looks prehistoric, like dinosaurs should start marching down one of the hills. As we stand on this pile of trash, I put my hand up to shield my eyes from the sun.

Puente Hills has its own entrance off the freeway, so the trucks don't bother residents of nearby homes in Hacienda Heights, an upscale neighborhood. The view from Joe's car window on the way up had been of giant truck tires on their way into the landfill. Waste Management trucks, with their familiar green-and-yellow interlocking WM logo, grunt and rumble by the dozen. From my position in the passenger seat of Joe's sedan, surrounded by these giant trucks, I felt like I was on safari; the smaller trucks, holding between four and six tons of garbage, yield to the larger ones, which each carry up to twenty tons (about the weight of six Hummers). On average, 1,500 of these trucks thunder through here every day, starting at 6:00 A.M. In the largest landfill in the country, where everything is bigger, my whole sense of scale is off.

Some of the trucks have driven more than forty miles to get here, since Puente Hills is one of the most inexpensive places to unload. Civilians can dump their trash here as well, for $20 per pound, versus the $75 charged at other local landfills. Puente Hills only accepts solid waste materials—nothing hazardous, no paint or car oil. Truck drivers are held responsible for the acceptability of their loads. If this seems unfair, Joe says, the drivers know which of their customers do and don't follow the rules—they "know the good and the bad housekeepers." Five to ten trucks per day are randomly pulled over for inspections and drivers face fines or banning for violations. With its reputation for cheap rates, Puente Hills often reaches its maximum daily capacity of 13,000 tons by noon, and spends the rest of the day turning away trucks filled with homeless, wandering garbage.

Joe and I are off to another mountain on the west side of the landfill, facing the 605 freeway, where we park again at the peak. We look around at more brown sameness, more lack of obvious garbage. What's not buried beneath us are tires. In Puente Hills, two hundred tires pile up every day. Across America, we throw out about 270 million tires every year, and tires can't be buried in landfills. Joe said they had to learn this the hard way—they'd bury a tire, and ten or fifteen years later, it would inch itself up through all the garbage buried on top of it until it emerged from the heap. His other main concern in the landfill is seagulls, many thousands of which circle the area. He says they used to be quite a bother, squawking like they're diving for dropped boardwalk fries at the Jersey Shore, but today, I only see two of them, and they're quiet. Long black strings that look like telephone wires hang overhead; Joe's not sure why, exactly, but these seem to scare the birds off, at least for a while. Plastic grocery bags are a problem, too, since they catch the wind and can blow out of the landfill. A bag dancing in the air is a nuisance to Joe, and it reminds me of that now-cliché scene from *American Beauty* where the dancing bag is supposed to be a thing of beauty; that director has certainly not been to Puente Hills.

The overwhelming thing to consider, when you consider trash, is that we're making more and more of it by the year. From 2002 to 2006, the annual amount of trash America produced rose by 5.5 percent, from 483 million tons to 509 million tons. In a survey of thirty-nine states, thirty reported that landfill capacity was being added to handle our ever-growing trash piles.

So where does it all go? A joint study by BioCycle and the

Earth Engineering Center of Columbia University found that 64.1 percent of our waste is sent to landfills. As for the rest, 28.5 percent of our municipal solid waste is recycled and composted, and 7.4 percent incinerated, often in waste-to-energy plants. Divided by region, New England sends the smallest percentage of its trash to landfills, only 36 percent; the mid-Atlantic region does the next best, sending 49 percent of its trash to landfills. The ones who send the most: the Midwest, which dumps 77 percent, topped only by the Rocky Mountain region, which landfills 85 percent of its trash. With lots of open space, there's more room to bury trash, and the distance not to have to be constantly reminded of it, which is likely why less densely packed, larger states send more to landfills. Many of them also don't convert that waste to energy; while New England directs 35 percent of its trash into waste-to-energy programs, the Midwest does so for only 1 percent, and the Rocky Mountain region does even less than 1 percent. Not surprisingly, money also plays a huge role in whether trash ends up in landfills or recycled. Oklahoma, part of the region where 77 percent of trash ends up in landfills, is the cheapest place to dump trash, at $18 a ton; that's compared with the other extreme, Vermont, which sends only 36 percent of its trash to landfills, probably in large part because it costs around $85 a ton to dump there.

Why do we make so much trash in the first place? "We are a rich society, we can afford to buy things and use them only briefly," says Elizabeth Royte, author of *Garbage Land*. "We have an incredibly sophisticated advertising industry telling us that red isn't 'in' anymore; now get a blue one. Or change the shape of your fridge. We are trained from a very early age to pay attention to what is fashionable and we have to keep up—and that is uniquely American.

"We can afford to buy and toss; it's part of our culture. Other wealthy countries don't have as much room. For example, European homes are much smaller, and Parisian streets are too narrow for oversized SUVs. This whole 'bigger is better' attitude just doesn't seem to be as pervasive. Perhaps Europeans are more sensible about the environment because they have already run out of room to bury things—there isn't enough room to buy larger and larger things. To save space, you are not allowed to bury anything organic, like food, in landfills in the European Union, and they do a lot of incineration. Still, there just isn't enough room to get rid of the stuff, which means there is less of a disposable culture and more value is placed on quality."

Joe, now in his sixties, was part of the first class to graduate with master's degrees from Stanford in what is essentially the science of landfills. They had a choice for their diplomas to say Environmental Engineering, which Joe selected, only because he thought Sanitary Engineering "sounded like a degree in being a janitor." A man who could've studied communications or chemistry, he is articulate and erudite. However, in conversation, he requires constant corralling. Otherwise, his comments leap and zig in a way that is simultaneously endearing and frustrating. First, he's talking about a story on self-mutilation he heard on NPR this morning. "I can't understand why anybody would do that," he says. Then, with no segue, he'll say, "There are three kinds of smells in a landfill. The first is old trash, which smells rancid and sulfuric because it's free of oxygen. The second is . . . oh, do you see those silos over there? Those still have Nike missiles in them from the 1950s to shoot down Russian bombers." I will never know the second or third smell in a landfill, or what this has to do with self-mutilators, or why no one ever took the missiles away. Joe is so filled with ideas and facts and numbers that he seems to speak only in bursting, tightly packed sentences, rarely in paragraphs, and certainly never in pages.

He may be ready to move on from his job, but that doesn't mean he can't still find fun in garbage. He and I drive inside the tipping-room floor, where the trash from commercial loads is dumped onto the floor, sorted, and separated. When the trash piles up, air freshener sprays from the ceiling. The trash is sorted and then pushed into a row of holes along the floor for it to be baled. When it's empty, as it is now, having just finished sorting a load, the stadium-sized building's smooth, gray floors and domed ceiling make it feel as if I'm a player inside a monstrous air hockey table. The floor sparkles like it's ready to host a ballroom dancing competition, not thirteen tons of putrid-smelling garbage. Driving through the tipping-room floor, Joe cuts the wheel of his beat-up Cadillac, sending it into tight donut spirals.

"I love doing this!" Joe shouts, as if his grin didn't make this apparent. "Woo-hoo!"

He holds down the horn, and the sound reverberates endlessly in the empty room.

"Helloooooo!" he shouts out the open window, his voice echoing back for five whole seconds, again and again.

"Try it," he insists.

So, losing whatever journalistic credibility I may have established with him, I stick my head out the window, too.

"Hellooooooo!" I shout, my voice reverberating through the room.

There aren't many alternatives for what to do with our mountains of trash. It would cost $45,000 per pound, says Joe, to shoot trash into space. Every day, 108,234 tons of waste is incinerated, pumping potentially hazardous chemicals into the air. "Though they are very much improved from the smokestacks of ten or twenty years ago, incinerating still releases small amounts of lead and mercury," says Royte. "But it doesn't make trash disappear. It does reduce its weight by 75 percent, but you're still left with the ash. Because of the Clean Air Act, the ash goes into landfills and all the toxins that were kept out of the air go into the ground instead."

If that sounds bad, we're doing just as poorly by our oceans, dumping fourteen billion pounds of trash into them worldwide. Some of that is refuse from ships and old fishing gear, but only about 20 percent. The other 80 percent comes from land, mostly lightweight trash like plastic that rolls to the lowest point and floats down rivers until it winds up in the ocean. The strong surface currents of the North Pacific Gyre draw in waste material from North America and Japan, pulling it across the North Pacific Ocean. That's created what scientists call the Great Pacific Garbage Patch, a floating trash island that weighs 3.5 million tons. It was discovered in 1988, though oceanographers think it began forming in the 1950s. The mass is made up of 80 percent plastic, the final resting spot for about 2.5 percent of *all* plastic items made since 1950. The Garbage Patch has only expanded since then, floating in the rarely traveled ocean between San Francisco and Hawaii, and is now estimated to be about twice the size of Texas. In this mass, the concentration of plastic is seven times higher than the concentration of plankton, which isn't good news for sea creatures. Even more troublesome is that as the plastic breaks down into smaller floating particles, it begins to resemble plankton, which means that animals like sea turtles, jellyfish, and albatrosses consume it, which may ultimately kill them—not to mention the plastics entering the food chain via fish and birds, meaning humans may eventually consume our own trash. "What goes into the ocean goes into these animals and onto your dinner plate. It's that simple," says Dr. Marcus Eriksen, research director of the U.S.-based Algalita Marine Research Foundation.

At this point, winds and currents have trapped so much trash that oceanographers think it would be nearly impossible to even remove the island. "There's nothing we can do about it now except do no more harm," says Eriksen. Chris Parry, the public education program manager for the California Coastal Commission, agrees: "At this point, cleaning it up isn't an option. It's just going to get bigger as our reliance on plastics continues. . . . The long-term solution is to stop producing as much plastic products at home and change our consumption habits," such as using fewer plastic bags and bottles, and less packaging in the first place.

It seems we hit the earth with trash from every angle: burning it into the air, dumping it into the oceans, and burying it underground, where it might also pollute the groundwater. Biodegradable products and recycling are definitely great options, but what about all the stuff we use that's not reusable?

Royte suggests "extended producer responsibility"—basically, bringing those items back to the manufacturer. "Right now manufacturers make things and their responsibility ends once we buy it," she says. "Moving that waste to a landfill is the responsibility of taxpayers and whether you bought the product or not, you may live along the truck route, you breathe the air polluted by the incinerator, you use the groundwater and soil the landfills are potentially contaminating; we are all bearing the burden of disposing product waste. Making manufacturers responsible for dealing with the refuse will give them a strong incentive to build products that last longer, are made with fewer toxic materials, and are easier to take apart for recycling."

If it seems unlikely we could just hand our used stuff back to the company, it's working in the European Union, where many manufacturers take back their cars and computers to extract what they're able to recycle. Meanwhile, in the United States, it's completely legal in most places to throw out a cell phone or a computer monitor. But it's dangerous for those kinds of circuit boards to end up in landfills; for example, an item like a computer monitor contains heavy metals like mercury, copper, beryllium, and chromium, which can threaten the environment.

That said, it's difficult to ban common items if the town doesn't provide an alternative. "Saying 'no more compact fluorescents in a landfill' is not good unless there is another place where people can bring them to be handled responsibly," says Royte. "Same for places that don't allow yard waste—yes, landscaping debris like grass clippings clogs landfills, but if landfills stop accepting it, they should provide a composting station."

Back in the landfill, Joe is on his cell phone, trapped in "the voice mail system from hell." He hangs up and starts explaining why this dump isn't dirty, smelly, or rat-ridden. Each day's trash is piled into football field–sized cells, giant holes in the ground, at the rate of 1,200 tons of trash per hour. Bulldozers and compactors smash the trash to fill the extra space with even more trash, a stinky stew of used diapers, lo mein takeout boxes, empty Doritos bags, and gone-bad leftovers. When the cells are filled for the day, gigantic dirt movers cover the cells in a foot-deep mix of dirt and yard waste. The covering makes the underlayers of trash go anaerobic in less than two minutes, the chemical processes using all of the oxygen. So, without oxygen, roaches, rats, or any other living thing is almost instantly destroyed.

The layers are filled with eighty miles of pipes, two feet in diameter. They're used to pipe out the hazardous, highly explosive gases made by all the decomposing trash: methane (stinky, sulfuric) and carbon dioxide (odorless).

When Joe hangs up, I urge for linearity, so he makes a verbal flowchart of sorts. The pipes are connected to seventy-five miles of underground trenches, ultimately delivering the methane to the landfill's Gas-to-Energy Facility. There, the methane goes through four giant white trash can–looking smokestacks, where it's used to heat water until it converts into steam. The steam goes through turbines (kind of like windmills), which spin, turning a generator; the generator makes electricity. Naturally occurring gases from the landfill, similar to natural gas, create enough energy to power 70,000 homes per day. In 1994, the EPA formed the Landfill Methane Outreach Program under the United Nations Framework Convention on Climate Change. By capturing methane gas created by our trash and putting it to use, we can reduce greenhouse gas emissions while accessing fairly cheap energy. "You're taking what was a liability and turning it into an asset," Landfill Methane Outreach Program Team Leader Brian Guzzone told CNN.

Even after the landfill closes, the breakdown of trash will continue to produce gases to power these homes for the next twenty to thirty years. It's pioneering technology, and it was started right here by the Sanitation District engineers at Puente Hills. Nationally, there are around four hundred operational landfill gas projects. The EPA says two-thirds of the current projects are being used to generate electricity, producing approximately nine billion kilowatt-hours per year; the other third supplies gas for direct-use applications, such as fueling boilers, engines, and greenhouses. Combined, landfill methane in the United States produces the energy equivalent of electricity for 725,000 homes or enough energy to heat 1.2 million of them.

Joe and I get back in the car and drive on to the refrigerator graveyard. Puente Hills receives about fifty fridges every week: green ones, white ones, one with a sign still taped to it that reads FREE, MOTOR WORKS. Over to the right is a Pepsi vending machine and the font for the logo looks dated, late '80s or early '90s. Standing here, I feel like I'm wandering in time through Maytag showrooms from the 1960s to today. I see my grandmother's kitchen and my parents' kitchen and the kitchen in my rented apartment. This part of the landfill feels creepy, haunted, and desolate, such large and obvious abandonments.

It reminds me of an ad campaign from 2009 that showed beautiful, well-dressed women gazing at refrigerators that have trendy stainless steel doors. The breathy voice-over begins: "The only thing standing between you and your new LG French door refrigerator is . . . your old refrigerator." It then cuts to the women pushing their old (though still relatively new!) fridges off cliffs, tying them to railroad tracks, or going at them with chain saws.

Joe tells me the refrigerators' CFCs are bottled so they don't hurt the ozone. Puente Hills also salvages every part it can, an ethical code that's admirable in a way that feels refreshingly old-fashioned.

Still the PR guy, Joe rattles off another redeeming fact about the landfill. After Puente Hills reaches capacity, it will be grassed over and used as a park. The city guarantees it will never be used to build condos or a strip mall or anything industrial that will create even more waste. Puente Hills Sanitary Landfill will become Puente Hills Park, with trails for jogging, biking, and horseback riding. The National Solid Wastes Management Association argues that even while a landfill is open, the host community benefits from it, saying that the "fees, property taxes, license fees, and business taxes that a community receives from hosting a landfill have allowed for the elimination or substantial reduction in residential property taxes, construction of playgrounds and other recreational facilities, building new schools, hiring police and firemen, the purchase of new fire trucks and police cruisers, and making infrastructure improvements. Moreover, rather than reduce residential property values, these substantial community benefits should help to add value or at least reduce any marginal negative influence in the price-distance relationship of residential property to a landfill."

In fact, once Puente Hills Park opens, the landfill may actually *raise* the property values of nearby homes, which are part of what's already considered an upscale neighborhood. The closest homes to Puente Hills are 1,500 feet away; from the top of the landfill, none of them are even visible. Additionally, the landfill legally ensures the property value of these houses so the homeowners are guaranteed a return of at least what they spent. That's helpful, as there's no consensus about whether proximity to a landfill decreases home value. "Some studies indicate that landfills impose negative price effects while other studies offer positive effects," say Arthur C. Nelson, John Genereux, and M. Michelle Genereux, authors of the article "Price Effects of Landfills on Different House Value Strata" in the *Journal of Urban Planning and Development*.

Ultimately, though, they found "negative house price effects associated with landfill proximity" and that landfill price effects hit "higher valued homes disproportionately." The National Solid Wastes Management Association counters that there's no effect on home value, again citing fees and tax benefits communities receive by hosting a landfill.

It sounds like Puente Hills treats its neighbors well with its home value guarantee. It also allots seven hundred acres as a buffer between the trash and the surrounding neighborhood, and it landscapes so the mountain blends into the nearby canyon. I'd think this might make for some happy homeowners. But then, I'd be wrong.

Instead, it makes for messy arguments. Joe's represented Puente Hills at community discussions, what he calls "real California be-ins, where people practically cry and read poetry." He's heard the homeowners, whom he and Puente Hills work diligently to appease, complain "not in my backyard." He hears it so often he quickly refers to it by an acronym, NIMBY. That's just one from the list he keeps in his office when he needs to laugh. DIFF: do it for free. JMIGA: just make it go away.

"It helps to laugh," Joe says. "Better for the blood pressure."

But many of the people who have landfills in their backyards aren't laughing. A 1998 New York State Health Department study of people living near thirty-eight of the state's landfills found that women living within a thousand feet of a landfill faced a fourfold risk increase for bladder cancer and leukemia as women living farther away. That said, the researchers found no increase in incidences of cancer, for men or women, in the other five areas they studied: liver, lung, kidney, brain, and non-Hodgkin's lymphoma. Additionally, "Increases in risk of adverse health effects (low birth weight, birth defects, certain types of cancers) have been reported near individual landfill sites . . . [that] may indicate real risks associated with residence near certain landfill sites," noted a 2000 paper in the journal *Environmental Health Perspectives*. The authors also found "increased prevalence of self-reported health symptoms, such as fatigue, sleepiness, and headaches, among residents near waste sites have consistently been reported in more than 10 of the reviewed papers. It is difficult to conclude whether these symptoms are an effect of direct toxicologic action of chemicals present in waste sites, an effect of stress and fears related to the waste site, or an effect of reporting bias."

The 2005 debate in Kendall County, Illinois, over whether to allow a new landfill exemplified both the benefits and downsides. "Obviously, [a landfill] is not one of the most desirable things, but obviously we need to put our garbage somewhere," said the county's solid waste coordinator, Marlin Hartman (I like to think of him as the Joe of Illinois). On one hand, a landfill would bring the area between $1 to $3 million every year in host fee revenues. It would also provide the residents with guaranteed low-cost waste disposal for twenty years, versus paying to ship their trash to the state's other landfills. The Illinois Environmental Protection Agency reported that the existing landfills in the area would be at capacity in five years, and those in the entire state within twelve years; it could be especially beneficial for a town to have its own landfill as others fill up and stop accepting out-of-town trash.

The benefits sounded enticing. But then there were the risks. Even though modern landfills have a clay liner and plastic membrane, basically an industrial-strength diaper, to protect against dangerous leaks, there's still some potential for groundwater pollution. There's also "vapor coming off" the landfill, says Hartman, which may possibly pollute the air, even if the facility isn't incinerating. More truck traffic will clog roads (that's not the case for Puente Hills, Joe reminds me, because it has its own exit off the highway), not to mention bring unpleasant smells when those garbage trucks are rolling by. Then there's debris coming off the landfill, like those dreaded plastic bags, not to mention the infestation of birds, especially seagulls, trying to nab something to eat. But the final, and most serious, disadvantage, says Hartman, is what makes the decision so important: "Once you put in a landfill, it's there forever." Still, the county board decided to go ahead and started accepting applications from private landfill companies.

In more ways than just the sight and smell (both, it seems, relatively benign), I'm coming to terms with landfills. I'm also developing a real respect for the ones that seem to handle our trash problem so efficiently, like Puente Hills.

That's when Joe drops the news: Puente Hills is scheduled to close on November 1, 2013, when it reaches capacity.

"Where will all the new stuff go?" I ask, my voice panicked. "What are we supposed to do then?" My mind races through the possibilities. Will all that Los Angeles garbage pile up in front of the entrance to Cartier on Rodeo Drive, or maybe line the red carpet at the next Academy Awards? I sure doubt it. Trash is ugly, dirty, and smelly—thoroughly un-Hollywood. Most likely, Americans will continue producing trash in greater volumes than any other country—we make up 5 percent of the world's population, but 37.5 percent of its waste. We will also likely continue to demand we never see, smell, or have to think about our trash.

Joe looks straight ahead, silent. In nearly every city and town in America, we're paying the salary of someone like Joe to make our own stuff not our problem. We don't take much personal responsibility beyond dragging our garbage cans to the street twice a week. We are not responsible, or choose to take no responsibility, for the one main thing we can do: produce less trash. Joe (or his replacement) has to figure out how to do battle with the ever-growing mountain of refuse. Hanging out with him makes me feel like a bad dog; I find myself wearing an apologetically sheepish grin. Usually I don't think about my trash, and certainly not the people who have to deal with it. No wonder Joe is happy about retiring—he's had decades of this responsibility piled on top of him, smothering him daily. Every day, we create more and more of a problem, quickly overrunning our capacity, and look to him to fix it.

Joe still hasn't said anything, so I ask again, my voice higher with concern.

"Where will it all go?"

"I'm retired," he says. "It's not my problem."

The best thing to do about our trash—and also the most obvious, and the most difficult—is to produce less of it in the first place. One way to enforce this would be to charge people per pound to dump trash. If we did this, we'd probably be better trash producers, thinks Elizabeth Royte. "People would be a lot more careful about their purchasing decisions," she says. By cataloguing the waste her family produced every day, she learned to be a better shopper, buying items with less packaging or from farmers' markets or co-ops, with zero packaging. We'd be better about recycling, since separating recyclables would reduce our trash weight, and as a result, our costs. We'd also all start composting to get the heavy food waste out of our trash. She advises people to "think about what kind of waste something is going to make before you even buy it. Look at it on the shelf and say, 'Is it going to break soon? If it does, am I going to fix it? Will it become obsolete soon? Would it be toxic in a landfill?'"

"More than anything, we need to change our mentality," she says. "We need to get away from this culture of disposability and this idea that we can have whatever we want this instant and then toss it out without any thought of where it will go."

Right now, a lot of it still goes to Puente Hills, but only for a few more years. Though 70 percent of our country's refuse is buried in landfills, the landfills are closing at a rate of one per day, usually because they've reached capacity or the community put pressure on them to close by the agreed-upon date. We're producing more and more trash, but have fewer and fewer places to stash it. Take, for example, the years 1979 to 1995; during this time, Americans increased waste production by a staggering 80 percent. In that same span, the number of landfills in this country decreased by 84 percent. It is the kind of math that confounds. It makes me worry about what to do with my empty Starbucks cups from now on, a side effect that Joe tells me is common—but also temporary. When we "treat our front yards with the same care we treat our own living rooms," he will be happy. He thinks Americans tend to rely too heavily on the quick-fix solution. But, he says, if we keep producing waste at this careless rate without changing our behavior,

"It might be too late for a quick fix to work." He looks around at the mountain range, the artificial curves and peaks.

"Most societies fail because of mismanaged resources," Joe says, "and right now, we're mismanaging our resources."

II.

MEET THE FREEGANS

On this cold January night, I'm at the grocery store, doing my Sunday night shopping for the week. But tonight, rather than roaming the aisles, I'm digging through the trash. I'm here with a line of people, searching through bags the store put out for the garbage truck. The air is too cold for me to smell anything when we open the industrial-sized black bags lining the midtown Manhattan sidewalk, which turns out to be a good thing, because I can feel a lot of squished-up bananas in there. People walking by either pretend we're not here, this group of scavengers rooting through garbage bags, or they give us looks, ranging from concern to annoyance. Any other night and I would've been one of those people. But tonight, I'm with the freegans.

Freegans are urban foragers. Generally, their philosophy is that our economy and businesses are founded on waste and produce more goods than we'll ever need or even be able to consume. Their solution is to live—comfortably, most of them insist—off of our cultural detritus. That way, they don't create any more need, from the water that grows our crops to the fuel used in transporting them to the materials that have gone into packaging all of it. Rather than protesting, freegans have simply removed themselves from the economy. They do that by not paying for anything they don't have to—food, furniture, transportation (through ride shares or hitch-hiking), and even housing (through squatting). The group's literature on their Web site often sounds both lofty and angry: "Affluent societies produce an amount of waste so enormous that many people can be fed and supported simply on its trash. As freegans we forage instead of buying to avoid being wasteful consumers ourselves, to politically challenge the injustice of allowing vital resources to be wasted while multitudes lack basic necessities like food, clothing, and shelter, and to reduce the waste going to landfills and incinerators. . . . Despite our society's stereotypes about garbage, the goods recovered by freegans are safe, useable, clean, and in perfect or near-perfect condition, a symptom of a throwaway culture that encourages us to constantly replace our older goods with newer ones, and where retailers plan high-volume product disposal as part of their economic model."

Tonight's group of freegans is made up of eight people, three men and five women. Their ages span from twenty to fifty years old, and all are employed. None of them look like the kind of person who got dressed, or ate dinner, from a Dumpster. Nonetheless, here they are, peering into the line of a dozen clear garbage bags, calling out their finds ("Bagged arugula salad!") before digging in.

I ask if Cindy's around, and a woman points her out, bent over, a few bags down. Cindy is in her early thirties and thin, with smooth skin, ruddy tonight from the cold. She has a sweetly upturned nose, feral eyebrows, and wears a fuzzy green fleece vest over a black hooded sweatshirt. We'd been e-mailing through www.freegan .info, a Web site for freegans around the world, when she set me up with which grocery stores they hit and at what time.

"Welcome," she says, handing me an empty plastic bag, which she explains is for collecting the stuff I want to bring home. "There's lots to go around. Just don't take more than you need."

* * *

I feel an instant guilt wave thinking back to my meal the night before, when I took so infinitely more than I could ever need. My family—my parents, brother, uncle, and grandmother—could not get up from the table. We were moaning and clutching our stomachs and tugging on the waistbands of our pants, wishing they were elastic. Much to my mother's dismay, there was burping. It was only 3:00 P.M., and yet we'd all have happily napped under the table. We had just eaten lunch at Harold's New York Deli Restaurant, which is not in New York but actually Edison, New Jersey. It was started by one of the founders of Manhattan's renowned Carnegie Deli, and one of my grandmother's friends from her Jersey neighborhood raved about it, so there we were. My grandmother especially wanted to come because she was fascinated by the chocolate éclair, one of her favorite desserts, that her friend said was massive. (It was indeed massive, more dessert than my ninety-one-year-old grandmother could probably eat in six months. It was also $16.) I wasn't sold on going until we arrived and I saw the sign boasting WORLD'S LARGEST PICKLE BAR.

But my biggest source of guilt is inspired by a pile of sliced turkey. My dad and I decided to share a sandwich, since we'd heard Harold's portion sizes were huge; the turkey sandwich arrived as a stack of twenty-six ounces of meat and a mountain of sliced rye bread, so there was an almost unnerving amount left over.

"Let's get this wrapped up for you," my dad said. "You can make it into a sandwich for lunch every day this week."

I smiled and nodded, because I knew the thought of me industriously reusing would make him happy and feel like the leftovers from the $33 he'd spent on this sandwich would actually continue to feed me. And probably, they could. But, to my own embarrassment, the thought of having to buy a loaf of bread, Ziploc baggies, lettuce, and tomatoes was enough to make me think twice. I knew that, realistically, if I carried the parcel of turkey home on the train with me from this restaurant in New Jersey to my apartment in Manhattan, and dutifully placed it in my fridge, that's exactly where it would stay for the next few days. I knew that, heart heavy with guilt, I'd just throw it out a few days later, haunted by the mantra of all nagging mothers: "But people are starving somewhere!" I'd just feel like a jerk.

So I decide to spare myself the hassle. As my family stood up and made their way past the display cases of giant cakes and toward the restaurant's exit, I pretended to forget the wrapped-up turkey on the table. Tonight, on my hands and knees on this frozen January sidewalk, up to my elbows in garbage bags of perfectly good food, I think about the wastefulness of leaving behind that giant stack of turkey. And though it was an unusually excessive, wasteful meal, there have certainly been plenty of others like them. I can't even start to think about how many garbage bags I've filled with my own wasted food.

It's that kind of waste that has made this movement of urban dwellers possible. They have taken the elimination of food waste to another level—adopting a hands-on way of ensuring that those old scraps don't wind up in our nation's landfills. I'd learned about them, and in fact met a few several years ago, and heard their talk about the wasteful consumer culture. But I'd never explored what it meant for them to be living, as they claimed to do, at zero-impact. Were the freegans, who have taken living small to an art form, on to something?

Cindy, positioned in a squat to root through the garbage bag next to me, lays down the rules.

"Don't block the sidewalk," she says, gesturing to the row of bags. "If we block the sidewalk, the store will start putting the bags in a locked Dumpster, or worse, compacting them."

As if on cue, a service door swings open and out comes a grocery store employee. He swings the bag back for momentum and throws it, hard, in Cindy's direction.

"Some employees are friendlier to us than others," a middle-aged Indian man in the group tells me.

Cindy bends down to check out the new bag's contents.

"The other rule is that we have to leave this place as clean or cleaner than when we got here," she says, like they're the Boy Scouts. The store gets fined if there's trash all over the street, which could lead to the store calling the police. "That means untie the bags, never rip them open. And then retie nicely," she says.

I nod, but I'm having trouble paying close attention, since every few words people are calling out their finds, like produce Tourette's syndrome: "A bag of Dole bananas!"; "A yellow pepper with a 'grown in Holland' sticker!"; "Tomatoes!"

Americans waste about 27 percent of our food. I know that moms aren't joking about people all over the world starving while we waste, but as a child, I could never understand why me eating (or not eating) my peas had anything to do with someone in the Sudan. If I ate the peas, I figured, they'd go into my body; if I didn't, they'd go in the trash or in our border collie's bowl. What difference did it make? But the Department of Agriculture estimates that recovering just 5 percent of the food that we waste in America could feed four million people a day. The United Nations says our leftovers could satisfy every single empty stomach in Africa.

During the Clinton administration, then–Secretary of Agriculture Dan Glickman implemented a program to get hospitals and schools to donate unused food and farmers to donate leftover crops, but it was discontinued by the Bush administration. Food that's not in shape to be eaten could be composted (as the city of San Francisco does) or used to feed livestock, but in most places, it's still just headed to rot in landfills. Twelve percent of all the nation's waste is food. We toss thirty-eight million tons of food annually, according to the Environmental Protection Agency. I always figured it wasn't so bad to throw out organic materials, but I also never thought of them as taking up space in a landfill, though that's exactly where 98 percent of food waste ends up.

I'm sure we could stand to buy less at the grocery store, order less at restaurants, and generally have less to waste in the first place. As the portions at Harold's suggest, it may not be a good life strategy—or a good waistline strategy—to eat everything on your plate simply to avoid wasting it. In a country where 66 percent of us are obese, isn't it wise, even a heroic act of sheer willpower, to toss out that half-full box of s'mores-flavor Pop-Tarts?

At the Whole Foods Market near my apartment, the trash area is divided into different sections, one for recycling glass, another for plastic, and so on. The things that don't fit into any recycling category go into a hole marked "Trash—Landfill." It causes me—and perhaps is meant to cause me—almost physical pain to toss 90 percent of my lunch remnants into that chute. In some ways it's unnerving to know freegans are going through my trash, seeing everything I deemed unnecessary. But it's also comforting to think that someone is going through my trash and taking what could be of value. It's reassuring in a way to know the freegans are out there, especially where I live, so I can still hope someone might be reclaiming my junk and putting it to good use. The idea of supporting freeganism with my trash (though not being a freegan) is so appealing because it's the lazy man's activism.

"Though official figures are hard to come by, freegan ranks are believed to be in the thousands, with an estimated five hundred practitioners living in New York City alone," wrote Jan Goodwin in the 2009 article "She Lives Off What We Throw Away." "Born of the extreme environmentalist and anti-globalization movements of the '90s, freeganism is a wholly modern crusade whose followers live off the grid while simultaneously exploiting it." It's no surprise that, living in New York City, I could use www.freegan.info to find a group of foragers and join them that very day. Goodwin also found that "Freegans gravitate toward cities—and their relentless mounds of garbage; Web sites keep devotees in close contact with each other so they can plan group foraging outings, recruit new members, and spread word of upcoming events, like move-out day at a college dorm, a veritable freegan Christmas."

There are basic health guidelines that most freegans follow.

"I don't do meat, since that's what can turn bad the quickest," says one of the foragers in our group.

"If it looks bad, don't eat it," says another, who eats meat. "If it smells off, looks weird, or tastes a little funny, I don't mess with it."

Especially if the food is just put out, rather than sitting out all day, most health experts also don't see foraging as a major safety concern.

"Freegans have been living this way for years and are very healthy," says Dr. Ruth Kava, director of nutrition at the American Council on Science and Health. "In fact, a freegan's biggest risk may be falling headfirst into a dumpster."

Actually, a bigger problem for freegans than is-it-or-isn't-it-spoiled milk is the threat of being busted for trespassing. Lila, a wiry, recent New York University grad with doe eyes, tells me how much better it is to forage in trash bags on the street rather than those in a Dumpster.

"The sidewalk is public property, so technically if we don't cause any trouble, we're allowed to be here," she says, "But they usually keep Dumpsters in parking lots or behind the store—basically on private property, so they can always kick you out for trespassing."

She tells me about a recent incident. "I was with a friend, going through the Dumpster behind the Brooklyn Trader Joe's. I didn't make a mess at all—I just jumped in and started filling up my bag with a bunch of potatoes and onions. Then all of a sudden a guy comes out of the store yelling that he's a manager and he's going to call the cops on us for trespassing and stealing, so we jumped out and ran off. But I still don't see why they care. They obviously didn't want that merchandise—it was in their trash—so why do they care if I take it? How on earth is that stealing?"

Store owners often don't want to take the risk of freegans getting hurt on their property, especially since eating expired food or crawling inside a metal container filled with garbage sounds like high-risk behavior. That's why lots of grocery stores lock their Dumpsters or compact their refuse. In 2006, two men were arrested in Steamboat Springs, Colorado, after jumping a fence behind a health food store and taking five cucumbers, four or five apricots, two bundles of asparagus spears, and a handful of cherries from a garbage can; they were charged with felony second-degree burglary and misdemeanor theft. They were finally freed when they accepted a deal and pleaded guilty to misdemeanor trespassing, agreeing to a six-month jail sentence to avoid a felony conviction.

"The Whole Foods near my apartment compacts everything," says Lila. "It's so sad. If they're worried about getting sued if I get hurt, I'd be happy to sign a release. I just don't understand why, especially with a company that says it's so into helping the community and being green, they would still rather waste all of that food."

My fingers are frozen into little Popsicles, and I've got some un-identifiable gunk on my hand. Only two people in the group are wearing gloves. The Dumpster divers I knew in college seemed somehow less gritty than this. I remember them riding their bikes to the rows of Dumpsters behind restaurants, and how they'd yell "Jackpot!" when they'd unearth a plastic bag full of thirty perfect-condition, day-old bagels. Though I hung out with them for their adventures, I never ate from their catch. But I used to envy that, for that day at least, they'd proudly lived at zero impact, created no demand.

That's actually where I first heard the term "freegan." I was hang-ing out with an acquaintance from the Dumpster diving group whom I knew to be a vegan—she didn't eat any animal products, even go-ing so far as to ban honey. But as we sat down one day with a big group of friends, circled around a few boxes of pizza, I saw her reach for a slice of pepperoni after everyone had finished eating.

"When did you stop being vegan?" I asked. She'd worn the dietary descriptor like a badge of honor, so I was surprised she'd given it up.

"I'm not vegan anymore. I'm a freegan now," she said.

She explained: "It's from the words 'free' and 'vegan.' So I don't buy meat or dairy products," she said. "But if something's free,

I'm not buying into the corporate system, so it's like home base—
it's a safe zone."

I still didn't get it. Did she eat meat or not?

"I can't be a freegan and buy a hamburger," she said. "I'd be
supporting deforestation in Argentina to make more cattle pas-
ture, and I'd be supporting factory farming and the cruel ways
they slaughter cattle, and I'd be giving money to McDonald's,
who doesn't pay a living wage."

I nodded. No burgers; got it.

"But if *you* bought a McDonald's hamburger, and then you ate
half of it and you were gonna throw it out, I could eat it, no penalty,
because I wasn't creating a new need for it," she said, reaching for
another slice of pizza. "In fact, it's being more environmentally
friendly for me to eat it than if I didn't and it ended up in a landfill."

Sometimes I'm reminded of her and the rest of the Dumpster
divers I used to know. I think of how they would've considered
where I live a treasure trove, since my apartment building is two
doors down from a busy upscale Italian restaurant that lines the
street every night of the week with more than a dozen trash bags of
produce, fish heads, and stale baguettes. Sometimes I wonder:
Could I counter my instances of food wasting—and the accompa-
nying guilt—by eating as much "found" food? If I couldn't do it
when I was eighteen and thought Dumpster divers were cool,
could I now, nearing thirty and with a respectable job (at a *fashion*
magazine for God's sake), bring myself to eat garbage if it meant
significantly minimizing my impact? I decided to find out.

Next to the bakery, the trash bags are stuffed and poking out in all
kinds of weird shapes. Cindy massages the bags to discern which

ones are filled with regular trash, like messy coffee grounds, and which have loaves of bread and bagels. She finds one nearly bursting with challah, the braided Jewish bread that was on my family's dinner table every Friday night when I was growing up.

"These look perfectly fine," I say. "Why are they here?"

"They are fine," she says. "If you'd have been here an hour ago, you would've been paying for this food. But it's the end of the day, and they need to get rid of the food that's marked 'sell by' today's date. They need to bake new bread tomorrow.

"When I was a kid," Cindy goes on, "every bakery sold half-price day-old bagels, You could buy bruised produce that would be bagged together, sold for soup stock. But they don't have either of those anymore at most places. I mean, who makes their own broth from scratch anymore anyway?"

I admit I never have. But for Cindy, it's bigger than soup.

"The reason there's all this wasted food is because of the myth that frugality doesn't matter anymore," she says. "It's also the American myth of plenty, that we have so much we'll never run out and that we'll always be able to afford more."

With that, she pulls another challah from the trash bag and hands it to me. The bread is exactly as it should be: dense and doughy, light golden yellow. I put it in my plastic bag and stand around while the freegans transfer muffins, donuts, and hoagie rolls from the big black bags into their own take-home bags.

We hit another grocery store that's just closed for the evening, whose bags are filled with bell peppers, red and white onions, sliced shrink-wrapped trays of Portobello mushrooms, zucchini, bags of shredded carrots. One bag is filled with "smushed banana goo," according to one of my companions, and is quickly retied. They find a few prepared ready-to-eat dinners of turkey, gravy, and mashed potatoes. Seeing meat in the trash makes Cindy more up-set than produce, bread, or anything else.

"That animal was raised specifically for the purpose of being consumed by us. It endured inhumane factory-farming condi-tions, and then it was slaughtered. And what was all that for? To end up in the garbage?"

It's now 11:30 at night and way below freezing. I say good-bye to Cindy, who asks if I've gotten enough food.

"Yup," I say, holding my CVS drugstore bag filled with Dump-ster challah.

I duck around the corner so the freegans won't see me hail a taxi instead of dutifully taking the subway. After one pulls up and I jump in, we stop-and-go for the thirty-some blocks to my apart-ment. I try to take in the whole experience.

I pull the challah from the bag and sniff it. It smells fine—good, in fact. It's dry to the touch, not covered in trash juice. I want to eat it. It smells good, was made fresh a few hours ago, and is one of my favorite foods—not to mention the fact that it might appease some of my guilt for throwing out so much usable food earlier this week.

My fingers pull the bread apart, digging into the soft ridges until I come away with a two-inch chunk. As I lift it to my mouth, my hand reflexively pulls away. *This is garbage,* my gut tells me. *Dirty germy trash food.* Yet I remind myself that this bread is only in the trash in the first place because we waste so much, not be-cause there's anything wrong with it. The cognitive dissonance is overwhelming. I lift the piece of bread to my mouth again, and before I can wimp out, I pop it in and chew. It tastes like the squishy, sweet bread I expected, though maybe a little tangier than

I remember. Momentarily I panic—is that because of some horrible deadly trash disease coating, or just this bakery's recipe?

In front of my apartment building, I pay the taxi driver. I walk up the four flights of stairs and, once inside, plunk my challah down on the kitchen table. I think that I should eat it for breakfast instead of buying something new (look at all the waste I'm not creating!). But it becomes clear to me that my brief stint as an urban forager is over.

Cindy and the freegans live small, so small that they arguably make zero impact on the environment. They claim that, meanwhile, they're making a huge impact by keeping their dollars out of a system they believe is critically flawed. "I'm literally not buying into it," Cindy says. But, as I riffle through my medicine cabinet to find some Pepto-Bismol—that challah, or at least my worry about it, is causing flips in my stomach—I realize that freegans are living at an extreme that is just as impossible to sustain as its living-large opposite.

As I pick up the challah and toss it into my trash can, I feel a twinge of guilt. I hope Cindy will understand.

EPILOGUE

In researching this book, I came across a bestseller from 1960 called *The Waste Makers* by Vance Packard. He asserted that post–World War II, America embarked on the "Throwaway Age," with most of us becoming "waste makers . . . as ever-greater consumption and wastefulness have become a part of the American way of life." As early as fifty years ago, Packard's book suggests, we began hurtling toward excess at breakneck speed—and we've only picked up steam in the '80s, '90s, and '00s. He says, "Wealth has made chronic optimists of the people of the United States. There has been so much wealth that they have come to assume there will always be more where that came from." Packard cites an early 1950s report by the President's Materials Policy Commission, which concluded: "The United States' appetite for materials is gargantuan—and so far insatiable."

That was fifty years ago. You can't help but wonder—when will we be sated? At what point in driving a bigger car or living in a bigger house or staying in a bigger hotel or shopping in a bigger mall do we finally say, "Okay, enough. I think we're good here"?

Freegans, who waste nothing and buy nothing, live so small their impact is microscopic. Their intentions may be noble, but were the trend to take hold (an unlikely scenario at best), the result would be anything but minor. Especially since 70 percent of the U.S. economy is based on consumer spending, it would be harmful—if not altogether disastrous—to propose that Americans follow suit and simply stop consuming.

When President Dwight Eisenhower was asked what Americans could do to fight the recession, he said, "Buy." When the reporter followed up with, "Buy what?" Eisenhower responded, "Anything." The sentiment was echoed by President George W. Bush decades later, facing another recession post-9/11, when he said, "I ask your continued participation and confidence in the American economy." In other words, according to a *Time* article on that speech, "For God's sake keep shopping." A *Washington Post* article called "How Did Spending Become Our Patriotic Duty?" noted that during World War II, when times were tough, millions signed this pledge: "As a consumer, in the total defense of democracy, I will . . . buy carefully. I will take good care of the things I have. I will waste nothing." The article makes the astute point that in the 2000s, we were told the exact opposite, that the best way for us to help our country was by buying, even to the detriment of the individual family's budget. "Patriotism normally suggests a willingness to sacrifice for the good of the nation—if not lives, fortunes and sacred honor, at least normal creature comforts," the article says. "But market patriotism suggests a strange kind of sacrifice: continue the binge we've been on for years." That our economy should crash years later seems like an unsurprising—if not *fitting*—answer to those shortsighted presidential pleas.

In some ways, the crash was a boon. We needed a new way of thinking about what it means to be an American, some greater call to duty than being asked to be big spenders. President Obama was on the mark when, just three weeks after being inaugurated, he announced, "The party's over." Of course, to celebrate that end would be to celebrate a failure with huge implications—that the country's banks and automakers are on the verge of collapse, that a record number of homeowners are on the verge of foreclosure, that countless thousands are unemployed.

But there may be some value in the pause it's given us. It allows us a moment to consider how we arrived at this place. It also gives us space to evaluate what kind of America we want to be when we come out of this mess, as we surely will.

I for one hope for a more sensible-sized America—that living large might come to connote having a rich, full, satisfied life, not one measured in square footage, carats, or horsepower. Packard wraps up *The Waste Makers* with this eloquent soliloquy: "Perhaps it is only natural that a people who have been so long overblessed with abundance will continue to squander and think in terms of ever-mounting strength—until a traumatic event abruptly forces them to realize that conditions now call for a more prudent and ingenious use of muscles and energy." It's a riff on boxer Eddie Shevlin's theory: "You can't learn anything until you're tired." Well, I'm tired of this. Aren't we all tired enough to try something new?

When the first few corporate giants started their layoffs, I was infuriated that instead of calling it "downsizing," they described the layoffs as "right-sizing." The euphemism seemed to gloss over the fact that people's careers and incomes had been lost in the process. But the more I thought about it, the more my affection grew for the term. Who says that going smaller—whether it means trading your SUV for a compact or two people moving from a six-bedroom home to a town house—has to be a step down? It could be a way to live a more streamlined life, but one where its content and experiences are more greatly appreciated.

Though the inner hippie in me cringes at the thought of

embracing corporate jargon, I suggest we reappropriate the term. If we can "right-size" our nation by thinking of the scaling back not as hard-times punishment but as a long-overdue readjustment, we can emerge from a difficult experience better-off—and that's something our industrious, supersized country is all about.

ACKNOWLEDGMENTS

I can't say enough thanks for the love and support of my family—especially my parents. Thank you for believing I could be a writer, despite reading my first book, written at age eight, a romantic comedy where the heartthrob's pickup line was, "You have a lot of body in your hair," and his crush responded with, "Enough to make another person?" Hopefully this book makes a little more sense.

Many thanks to my lovely friends, who didn't give up on me when I went on "social lockdown" to write and supported my project at every stage. I feel lucky to have the kind of friends who feel like family.

Thanks also to all of the contributors who endured my relentless interviews, drove me around, and let me eavesdrop in on their lives. Extra thanks to Amber Herczeg, Ryan Smith, and my mother, who were each very kind about me turning our vacations into research trips.

This book would never have become a book at all without three integral people. First, Yaniv Soha, my editor at St. Martin's Press, who shaped it at every turn with insight, precision, and patience—and occasionally spotted me a beer. Emmanuelle Alspaugh, agent extraordinaire, who worked tirelessly and believed in my voice from the beginning. Finally, Jeanne Marie Laskas, who first showed me that the writer's life could be a happy one and guided me through countless drafts and revisions. I'd also like to thank Joanna Coles and Lucy Kaylin at *Marie Claire* for their great encouragement and support of my writing; the same is true for Linda Wells at *Allure*. Thanks also to the English department at the University of Pittsburgh for seven years of transformative (and free!) education.

And though I'm 90 percent sure he can't read this, thanks to my dog, Ginsberg, for sitting by my feet through every chapter, giving me a reason to get outside when I couldn't bring myself to write another word.

SELECTED SOURCES

Adler, Margot. "Behind the Ever-expanding American Dream House." National Public Radio, July 4, 2006.

Ahmed, Kamal. "Google's Eric Schmidt on Why Bankers Deserve Little Sympathy and Obama Does." *The Telegraph*, January 9, 2010.

Ahrens, Frank. "The Hummer's Dead End?" *The Washington Post*, June 4, 2008.

Arieff, Allison. "How Green Is Your Brand?" *The New York Times*, June 16, 2008.

Barbaro, Michael. "Anxiety for Luxury Brands as Tiffany Reports Slowdown." *The New York Times*, January 12, 2008.

Barrick, Audrey. "Americans' Religiosity Not Impacted by Recession." *The Christian Post*, March 23, 2009.

Berton, Justin. "Continent-size Toxic Stew of Plastic Trash Fouling Swath of Pacific Ocean." *San Francisco Chronicle*, October 19, 2007.

"Big-business Bankruptcies Swamp Smaller Companies." *Chicago Tribune*, June 14, 2009.

"Big Gems, New Cuts, New Metals Popular; Local Jewelers Identify Trends." *The Post-Tribune*, February 3, 2008.

"Big Idea, Small Detail." *Reader's Digest,* June 2009.

Chad, Norman. "In Vegas, It's Easy to Live XXL." *The Washington Post,* June 15, 2009.

Chen, Daniela. "Converting Trash Gas into Energy Gold." CNN, July 17, 2006.

Childs, Dan. "Retail Therapy: Does Sadness Mean Spending?" *ABC News,* February 8, 2008.

Chua, Jean, and Thomas Mulier. "Diamonds Are a Man's Best Friend as Rings Get Cheaper." *Bloomberg,* May 1, 2009.

Clements, Jonathan. "The Problem Is the Big House, Not the Small Salary." *The Wall Street Journal,* November 30, 2003.

Collins, Glenn. "For Las Vegas Chefs, the Odds Grow Longer." *The New York Times,* July 14, 2009.

Cook, Karla. "Peanut Recall's Ripples Feel Like a Tidal Wave for Some Companies." *The New York Times,* February 25, 2009.

Cox, Stan. "Big Houses Are Not Green: America's McMansion Problem." www.alterNet.org, September 8, 2007.

DeCarlo, Scott, and Brian Zajack. "The World's Biggest Companies." *Forbes,* April 2, 2008.

de la Merced, Michael J. "General Growth Properties Files for Bankruptcy." *The New York Times,* April 16, 2009.

"Disaster on a Stick: Snapple's Attempt at Popsicle World Record Turns into Gooey Fiasco." www.associatedpress.com, June 22, 2005.

Dolan, Matthew. "Industry's Big Hope for Small Cars Fades." *The Wall Street Journal,* March 23, 2009.

Faiola, Anthony, and Zachary A. Goldfarb. "China Tops Japan in U.S. Debt Holdings. Beijing Gains Sway Over U.S. Economy." *The Washington Post,* November 19, 2008.

Fishman, Charles. "The Walmart You Don't Know." *Fast Company,* December 19, 2007.

Flanders, John. "The World's Biggest Hotel—in Vegas." *The Times* (UK), April 26, 2008.

Fletcher, June. "Slowing Sales, Baby Boomers Spur a Glut of McMansions." *The Wall Street Journal,* June 19, 2006.

"Four Ways of Looking at a Bubble." *Reader's Digest,* May 26, 2009.

Furlong, Pauline. "With This Ring . . . ; The Modern Girl's Engagement Ring Has a Bigger Rock, Bigger Price Tag." *The Times & Transcript,* July 31, 2007.

Garreau, Joel. "Big Box & Beyond: Today's Temples of Consumption Don't Have to Be Tomorrow's Ruins. What's in Store?" *The Washington Post,* November 16, 2008.

Garrison, Jessica. "Call It L.A.'s Really Big Show. Despite Economic Hard Times, the Ultra-rich Build Mega-mansions." *Los Angeles Times,* June 12, 2008.

Gibney, Alex. "Big Business Can Be Hazardous to Your Health." *The Atlantic,* June 8, 2009.

Gladwell, Malcolm. "The Cellular Church: How Rick Warren's Congregation Grew." *The New Yorker,* September 12, 2005.

Gomes, Andrew. "Walmart Fights Kauai Ban on 'Big-box' Stores." *The Honolulu Advertiser,* July 14, 2007.

Grace, Kerry E. "Tiffany's Net Drops 76% on Restructuring Costs, Plunging Sales." *The Wall Street Journal,* March 23, 2009.

Guster, Chandra Temple. "The Ring's the Thing." *Birmingham News,* August 21, 2008.

————. "With This Bling: Weddings Get Sparkly." *Newhouse News Service,* September 2, 2008.

Harden, Blaine. "Big, Bigger, Biggest: The Supersize Suburb." *The New York Times,* June 20, 2002.

Hoak, Amy. "Many Say Goodbye to McMansions." *The Wall Street Journal,* January 27, 2009.

Hujer, Marc, and Gerhard Spörl. "Interview with California Governor Arnold Schwarzenegger: 'We Should Be Saying, Keep the Luxury Car.'" *Spiegel,* March 12, 2007.

"Is the Smart Too Mini for a Man?" *Men's Vogue,* April 2008.

Johnson, Ken. "A Landfill in the Eyes of Artists Who Beheld It." *The New York Times,* February 1, 2002.

Jones, Steven T. "Governor Hummer." *San Francisco Bay Guardian,* October 31, 2006.

JTA. "Reform Movement Tries Out Mega-Church Strategies." *The Jewish Daily Forward,* December 21, 2007.

Judt, Tony. "Europe vs. America." *The New York Review of Books,* February 10, 2005.

Kaiser, Emily. "At Least the Mall of America Is Recession Proof." *City Pages*, October 7, 2008.

Kamp, David. "Rethinking the American Dream." *Vanity Fair*, April 2009.

Knightly, Arnold M. "Permits Sought to Build World's Largest Hotel in Las Vegas." *Las Vegas Review-Journal*, January 7, 2009.

Krangel, Eric. "Obama's Antitrust Pick: Google Is the New Microsoft." *The Business Insider*, February 18, 2009.

Kuczynski, Alex. "Critical Shopper: A Story in Every Box." *The New York Times*, February 8, 2007.

Kumar, Vishesh, and Jeffrey McCracken. "Wave of Bad Debt Swamps Companies." *The Wall Street Journal*, February 13, 2009.

Kurczewski, Nick. "An American S.U.V. in Paris." *The New York Times*, June 4, 2008.

Laskas, Jeanne Marie. "This Is Paradise." *GQ*, April 2008.

Leahy, Kelly. "National Hummer Club." *Green Daily*, February 25, 2009.

Leinberger, Christopher B. "The Next Slum?" *The Atlantic*, March 2008.

Leonhardt, David, and Geraldine Fabrikant. "Rise of the Super-Rich Hits a Sobering Wall." *The New York Times*, August 20, 2009.

Linn, Allison. "Budget-Minded Brides Seek Discount Deals." www.msnbc.msn.com, July 12, 2007.

Lohr, Steve. "High-Tech Antitrust Cases: The Road Ahead." *The New York Times*, May 13, 2009.

Marimow, Anne E. "Montgomery Aims to Make Green Homes Mandatory." *The Washington Post*, April 23, 2008.

Martin, Andrew. "One Country's Table Scraps, Another Country's Meal." *The New York Times*, May 18, 2008.

Martin, Karen. "Engagement Ring Diamonds Getting Bigger." *The Advocate*, February 3, 2008.

"Men Jailed for Stealing Garbage Released Unexpectedly." *ABC News*, September 6, 2006.

Mieszkowski, Katharine. "The Short, Disgusting Life of the Hummer." www.salon.com, December 5, 2008.

Mindlin, Alex. "Some Shoppers Head to Supercenters." *The New York Times*, May 26, 2008.

Moynihan, Michael C. "Big Box Panic." *Utne Reader*, May–June 2008.

Mufson, Steven. "Corporate America's Icons Crumbling Under Global Recession." *The Washington Post*, March 6, 2009.

Mui, Ylan Q. "Bottled Water Boom Appears Tapped Out." *The Washington Post*, August 13, 2009.

"New Home Sizes Shrink with Recession." United Press International, January 9, 2009.

New York State Department of Health. "Health Department Releases Landfill Study." August 21, 1998.

"No, You Can't Save the Planet: The Smart Man's Guide to Going Green." *GQ*, July 2008.

"101 Uses for a Deserted Mall." *The New York Times*, April 4, 2009.

Packard, Vance. *The Waste Makers*. Philadelphia: David McKay Co., 1960.

Pellegrini, Frank. "The Bush Speech: How to Rally a Nation." *Time*, September 21, 2001.

Pollan, Michael. "Why Bother?" *The New York Times*, April 20, 2008.

Reddy, Sudeep. "Home Prices Declined at Record Pace in October." *The Wall Street Journal*, December 31, 2008.

Reich, Robert B. "How Did Spending Become Our Patriotic Duty?" *The American Prospect*, September 23, 2001.

Rocca, Mo. "Is It Okay to Hate McMansions Now?" www.news.aol .com, October 14, 2008.

Rodriguez, Cindy. "Teens with Wads of Cash Flex Spending Muscle." *The Boston Globe*, February 20, 2002.

Rogers, Teri Karush. "And Do I Hear $2 Million for That Condo? No? 1 Million? Sold!" *The New York Times*, February 25, 2009.

Rosenbloom, Stephanie. "Malls Test Experimental Waters to Fill Vacancies." *The New York Times*, April 4, 2009.

"Sad, Self-absorbed Shoppers Spend More." Associated Press, February 8, 2008.

"San Diego City Council Defeats Walmart Superstore Ban." Associated Press, July 10, 2007.

Scott, Tony. "Officials Hear Landfill Pros, Cons." *Ledger-Sentinel*, May 19, 2005.

Segal, David. "Our Love Affair with Malls Is on the Rocks." *The New York Times,* January 31, 2009.

Solomon, Christopher. "The Swelling McMansion Backlash." www .realestate.msn.com, May 25, 2009.

Solomon, Deborah, and Jonathan Weisman. "Decade of Debt: $9 Trillion." *The Wall Street Journal,* August 26, 2009.

Solotaroff, Ivan. "Rules of Engagement." *Modern Jeweler,* October 2007.

Sullivan, Andy. "Foreclosures Come to McMansion Country." www .reuters.com, April 7, 2008.

Symonds, William C. "Earthly Empires: How Evangelical Churches Are Borrowing from the Business Playbook." *BusinessWeek,* May 23, 2005.

Taub, Eric A. "Behind the Wheel: Ready for Its Hollywood Close-Up." *The New York Times,* May 11, 2008.

"Tiffany Reports Third Quarter Results." *Business Wire,* November 26, 2008.

"US Debt Clock Runs Out of Digits." *BBC News,* October 9, 2008.

Van Riper, Tom. "The World's Largest Malls." *Forbes,* January 15, 2009.

Vascellaro, Jessica E. "Yahoo, Google Recast Ad Alliance." *The Wall Street Journal,* November 4, 2008.

Vitello, Paul. "Bad Times Draw Bigger Crowds to Churches." *The New York Times,* December 13, 2008.

Wallechinsky, David. "Is America Still No. 1?" *Parade,* January 3, 2007.

Webb Pressler, Margaret. "Big-Box Stores Rule Top 10 List: Walmart's No. 1 Rank Shows U.S. Goes for Price." *The Washington Post*, July 11, 2004.

Weiss, Eric M. "Gas Prices Apply Brakes to Suburban Migration." *The Washington Post*, August 5, 2008.

Wells, David F. "The Temptation the Church Always Faces." *Tolle Lege*, July 16, 2009.

West, Judy. "Shaping the Future of Fresh Kills." *Penn Current*, March 31, 2005.

WWD Staff. "De Beers Doubles Up." *Women's Wear Daily*, November 18, 2008.

Yancey, Kitty Bean. "What's the Largest Hotel in the World?" *USA Today*, October 15, 2007.

Zerzan, Rebecca. "Five Beloved Traditions Invented to Make You Buy Stuff." *The Wall Street Journal*, April 28, 2009.

OTHER RESOURCES

Eastern Connecticut State University, Shopping Mall and Shopping Center Studies

www.freegan.info

Hartford Institute for Religious Research

U.S. Census Bureau